Easy
EASTERN COOKING

Easy
EASTERN COOKING

Ranse Leembruggen

Macdonald

A Macdonald BOOK

First publiished in Great Britain in 1986
by Macdonald & Co (Publishers) Ltd
London & Sydney

A member of the BPCC plc

British Library Cataloguing in Publication Data
Leembruggen, Ranse
Easy Eastern Cookery.
1. Cookery, Oriental
I. Title
641.595 TX724.5.A1

ISBN 0-356-10521-0

Filmset by Flair plan Photo-typesetting Ltd.

Printed and bound in Great Britain by
Purnell Book Production Limited, Paulton, Nr. Bristol.

Editor: Julie Dufour
Designer: Sarah Jackson
Production: John Moulder
Photographer: David Johnson
Stylist: Kit Johnson
Home Economist: Ranse Leembruggen
Indexer: Michèle Clarke

Macdonald & Co (Publishers) Ltd
Greater London House
Hampstead Road
London NW1 7QX

Contents

Introduction

Asia stretches from India to China, east towards Japan, south to the Philippines and then west encompassing Indonesia and the Malaysian peninsula. To compile a cookery book on what I feel is the world's greatest and most exciting cuisine is a daunting task. Asia covers sixteen countries. China being one of these has five major cookery schools, namely Cantonese, Shangtung, Szechuan, Fujian and Hunan. There are also a number of minor schools, such as Yang Zhou and vegetarian. Each of these schools would be a complete work in itself, and to select easy recipes from any one of them would not be indicative of the cuisine of China or Asia. The same would apply to each of the other countries of Asia, except one, which has in its cuisine flavours of all the countries of Asia and Europe – Indonesia.

Indonesia is an area in Southeast Asia consisting of no less than 13, 660 islands where 120 million people live. Romantically dubbed 'Morning of the World,' these islands were discovered early in the sixteenth century by traders from Portugal, Spain, Holland and Great Britain. The huge profits these countries gained by extracting spices from the islands, namely cloves and nutmeg, turned the Indonesian archipelago into the fabled Spice Islands.

Naturally enough in a country of such size and cultural diversity, each region has its own distinctive dishes. On the whole, however, the varying influences of immigrants and travellers (and there is evidence of European, Middle and Far Eastern changes) have only enhanced the inventiveness of local cooks to produce an assortment of richly spiced dishes using all the available ingredients. There is, therefore, a unique blend of styles and tastes adapted to suit local origins and flavours.

The Malay Peninsula and all the islands that form Indonesia and Southeast Asia share a tropical monsoon climate and large areas are extremely fertile. The seas are plentiful in fish and shellfish and are easily navigated. Almost every known spice is available in boatloads, transported from island to island, encouraging and allowing a mixture of culinary ideas, goods and recipes to circulate freely. Most Indonesians are followers of the Muslim faith and practices, and as such are forbidden to eat pig flesh, but in some parts of Indonesia where the people are Hindu, life revolves around religious settings and festivals where a whole spit-roasted pig is the main feature of a banquet. In most cases, although fish is plentiful, it is not an important part of the Asian diet. Fish is enjoyed in Indonesia, but beef, buffalo, eggs, pork and poultry constitute the major part of the diet.

Despite all of this – the differences in each colourful society, their habits, customs, environment, etc. – they still use the same ingredients and cooking techniques, and they generously offer whatever they can afford, with complete disregard for orthodoxy.

This lack of orthodoxy is a basic element of Indonesian cookery. For example, in India garlic and onions play an important part in cooking, but to an orthodox Hindu too much is considered impure. Meat and eggs are as unwelcome to the Brahmins, the pillars of Hindu society, as meat is to orthodox Buddhists. However, the mixture of these religions in Indonesia allows their followers to be much more relaxed about the business of eating and to bend the rules and their attitudes to religious customs. Seasonal and cyclical festivals associated with the planting and harvesting of rice are celebrated all the time in different parts of the archipelago, and these festivals, slotted alongside the more orthodox religious rituals, tend to make life for Southeast Asians a merry-go-round of festive occasions. Despite this, the serious business of work is never very far away.

Unless hard times have caught up with them, Asians expect to eat rice at least three times a day, even though there is little else to go with it. White rice is to the Asians what bread is to Europeans: a sign that they are at least holding their own above starvation level. Rice therefore plays an important part in the everyday life of Asians and features in their ceremonial rites. Its cooking, arranging and eating reflects this most closely, and it has always saddened me to see how badly this humble grain, so steeped in myth and mysticism and so necessary in Asia, is treated in countless Western kitchens.

Food must be shared, and shared in vast quantities. At any meal where guests are present, far more is put on the table than is necessary, and much more than the company can possibly eat. This is not a display of the host's wealth, but more to do with having plenty available for all, as the people of Southeast Asia have a charming habit of bringing friends or relatives along to any dinner party they have been invited to. So a simple dinner party for ten can easily stretch to twenty or thirty.

Eating in an Asian household is somewhat different to the European style as almost all the dishes are placed on the table together and you will then be asked to help yourself. In Europe, the hostess will regularly have to leave the table to fetch and carry each course, spends most of the evening taking part in disjointed conversations, and ends up worn out. The Dutch took the Indonesian form of eating as a base for their *Rijstaffel*, sampling each dish one at a time or mixing various dishes. Helping yourself to one or several more helpings is considered a compliment and an extremely polite way of saying you are enjoying your food. Most Asians generally eat with their fingers and, even if they are left-handed, only the right hand is used, as the left hand is considered unclean.

Tables are of course a Western invention. I spent the first six years of my life in the little Malay village of Sentul Pashar just outside Kuala Lumpur and at meal times sat cross-legged around the *'kuali'* on the eartheny kitchen floor, listening to the buzz of conversation and never, never taking my eyes off the mountain of food before me. These memories and my nomadic wanderings around the Far Eastern and European food centres have led me to write this book. I am aware that no cook can expect to reproduce exactly any of the dishes prepared in Asia, and it is not the intention of this book to do so. It is my intention, however, to offer readers a rewarding experience by guiding them to try a rich and diverse culinary tradition, and if this book achieves that goal, I shall be more than satisfied.

Selamat Makan!

Stocks

At one time, stockmaking was a complicated ritual. Pots of bones would simmer for hours, even days, to obtain a small quantity of a savoury, richly flavoured stock. Indeed, to produce a good sauce it is essential to have a stock that has been prepared with care and attention. However, with the advent of nouvelle cuisine, *and its infinite variety of light sauces with delicate flavours, the most desirable stocks have become relics of the past.*

In this book, stocks play an important part as the base on which the dish is built. As time is of the essence, lengthy stock making processes are not practical, but the stock must at least bear some resemblance to the original. All shops these days carry stock cubes of infinite brands and varieties; it is not enough to just dilute one of these to use as a base, but you can add to it, so that it does have some of the flavour of a good stock.

CHICKEN STOCK

Makes 1 litre/1¾ pints stock
Preparation time 15 minutes
Cooking time 2 hours

1 Bring the stock to the boil and remove any scum from the surface.
2 Add all the other ingredients and simmer gently for 2 hours.
3 Strain the stock through a fine cloth or sieve and season to taste.

25 g/1 oz chicken stock cube dissolved in 2 litres/3½ pints water
110 g/4 oz mushrooms, sliced
110 g/4 oz carrots, peeled and diced
1 onion, peeled and cut in half, studded with 1 clove
1 leek, sliced
1 stalk celery, diced
1 whole clove garlic, lightly crushed
1 sachet bouquet garni
salt and freshly ground pepper

BEEF STOCK

Make as above but substitute a beef stock cube for the chicken stock cube.

FISH STOCK

Makes 1 litre/1¾ pints stock
Preparation time 30 minutes
Cooking time 30 minutes

1 Heat the butter in a suitable pan, add the onion, leek and celery and cook for 2–3 minutes.
2 Add the fish bones, white wine and water, bring to the boil and remove the scum and fat by skimming with a perforated spoon.
3 Reduce the heat to simmer, add the parsley and thyme and cook for 20 minutes.
4 Strain through a cloth or fine sieve and season to taste. Set aside to cool.
5 When cool, pour into small containers to freeze. Use as required.
Note: This is a good way of making fish stock – the bones of white sea fish should be used and the fish must be fresh. If fresh fish is not available, use 25 g/1 oz fish stock cube dissolved in 1.2 litres/2 pints of water and introduce into your cooking method at step 2, leaving out the wine and water.

1 kg/2 lb fish bones and heads (gills removed)
25 g/1 oz butter
1 large onion, peeled and coarsely chopped
1 leek, white part only, sliced
2 stalks celery, coarsely chopped
150 ml/¼ pint white wine
1.2 litres/2 pints water
3 sprigs fresh parsley
2 sprigs fresh thyme or a pinch of dried thyme
salt and freshly ground pepper

Soups and Starters

Asian food is unquestionably some of the most delicious in the world. I may be slightly prejudiced in making such a bold statement, as most people tend to think of Asian food as hot, pungent and extremely spicy. I admit there is no subtlety about it, but what exhilaration for the taste buds! The combination of sweet and sour and salty tastes; fragrant and gentle spices; unexpected creamy coconut milk flavoured with lemon, lime or herbs; tiny quantities of hot sambal *with perhaps some crisp accompaniments and a bowl of soup: these are just some of the delights of this unusual cuisine.*

As a rule, starters do not play an important role at dinner during an Asian meal. It is more common for the whole meal to be put onto the table, including soups, and the guests to help themselves. Most of the recipes included in this section are considered as snacks and are eaten all the time. They are readily available everywhere, and on many a roadside there will be a little chap with a makeshift portable kitchen turning out an immense variety of snacks. He will be operating with no more than a tin drum containing hot coals, which he constantly fans into flame under an enormous kuali. *All the food is served or wrapped in banana leaves and, if you want soup, you must provide your own bowl. It is difficult to envisage this scene as you sit down to a traditional three-course meal, and when recreating the starters and soups for this section, I modified many of the recipes to suit Western eating habits.*

SOUPS

CHILLED COCONUT SOUP

For 4–6 people
Preparation time 10 minutes
Cooking time 15 minutes

I believe this soup, originally served hot, comes from somewhere in South India and has undergone many changes to result finally in this recipe.

570 ml/1 pint coconut milk, made with 350 g/12 oz desiccated coconut and 570 ml/1 pint milk (see page 105)
570 ml/1 pint chicken stock, made with 570 ml/1 pint water and 25 g/1 oz chicken stock cube
1 teaspoon mild curry powder
salt
1 tablespoon finely chopped chives

1 Heat the chicken stock to just below boiling point. Add the curry powder and blend in well. Set aside to cool.
2 When cool, add the coconut milk, season to taste with salt and refrigerate for several hours.
3 Just before serving, quickly blend again for about 5 seconds in a food processor or with a balloon whisk. Pour into chilled soup bowls, garnish with chives and serve immediately.
Note: For this unusual and very refreshing soup, it is worthwhile going to the trouble of finding a fresh coconut and also of making your own chicken stock. Also make sure that the coconut you buy contains a fair amount of liquid (check by shaking and listening) and, if it is sweet, add this liquid to the coconut milk.

SPINACH SOUP

For 6–8 people
Preparation time 30 minutes
Cooking time 25 minutes

The first time I tasted this soup, it was made with Chinese cabbage and served to me in a coconut shell. The colour of the soup didn't make it look too appetizing, but the smiling Dyak princess who served it more than compensated for the appearance of the soup. They were both delightful!

225 g/8 oz young spinach leaves, washed and roughly chopped
850 ml/1½ pints chicken stock (see page 9)
50 g/2 oz shallots, peeled and diced
2 cloves garlic, crushed
½ teaspoon turmeric
¼ teaspoon chilli powder
¼ teaspoon ground ginger
1 bay leaf
225 g/8 oz frozen or canned sweetcorn kernels

1 Put the chicken stock, shallots, garlic, turmeric, chilli powder, ginger and bay leaf in a suitable pan. Bring to the boil, turn down the heat to low and simmer for 10 minutes.
2 Add the sweetcorn kernels, bring the soup back to the boil and add the chopped spinach leaves.
3 Bring back to the boil, simmer for 3 minutes, then season to taste with salt.
4 Remove the bay leaf and serve immediately.

SPICED MEAT SOUP

For 4–6 people
Preparation time 30 minutes
Cooking time 1 hour 10 minutes

This is one of the Indonesian soups I could go on eating for ever. Every mouthful can be made original by adding one or more of the garnishes and following the serving instructions.

700 g/1½ lb stewing beef
1.2 litres/2 pints water
salt
110 g/4 oz prawns, raw or cooked
2 tablespoons vegetable oil
225 g/8 oz onions, diced
6 cloves garlic
½ teaspoon ground ginger
½ teaspoon turmeric
a pinch of chilli powder

Sambal
10 fresh red chillies
25 g/1 oz ground almonds
salt
55 ml/2 fl oz beef stock (see page 9)

Garnishes
4 spring onions, finely chopped
leafy ends of 2 celery heads, finely chopped
6 cloves garlic, peeled, deep-fried and thinly sliced
juice of 4 lemons or 6 limes

1 Put the meat into a deep pan, add the water and a pinch of salt. Bring to the boil, then turn down the heat and simmer for 30 minutes.
2 Remove the meat and cut into fine strips, then return the strips to the stock in the pan and set aside to cool.
3 Peel and clean the prawns, mash or chop them finely.
4 Heat the oil in a suitable pan, add the onions and sauté gently for 5 minutes, without browning. Add the chopped prawns and cook for a minute longer.
5 Add the garlic, ginger, turmeric and chilli powder and 275 ml/½ pint of the liquor in which the meat was cooked. Season with a little salt if necessary. Bring to the boil, cover and simmer gently for 10 minutes.
6 Strain the contents of this pan into the pan with the strips of beef and stock. Bring this back to the boil, turn down the heat and simmer for 15–20 minutes.
7 Meanwhile, make the *sambal*. Grind the red chillies in a pestle and mortar, mix in the ground almonds, a pinch of salt and the beef stock.
8 Transfer the *sambal* to a small pan and heat gently until the moisture has evaporated and the *sambal* is dry.
9 Put the beef soup in a large warm bowl and place on the table. Arrange all the garnishing ingredients, including the *sambal*, on separate plates or bowls around the soup, so each guest can place into their bowl as much vegetable or *sambal* as required, ladling the soup on top.
Note: The *sambal* is not absolutely necessary; without it the soup is still very good but not authentic. If fresh red chillies are not available, a teaspoon of chilli powder will suffice, or one of the brands of chilli sauce that are in most shops nowadays.

SOUR PRAWN SOUP

For 4–6 people
Preparation time 10 minutes
Cooking time 30 minutes

I believe this soup originated in Thailand. Its unique flavour is very popular among the Chinese population of Asia, hence the reason for its inclusion.

1 Bring the fish stock to the boil in a suitable pan. Add all the ingredients except the prawns and chives. Turn the heat down and simmer gently for 20 minutes.
2 Strain the stock into a clean pan, add the prawns and heat gently for 5 minutes.
3 Serve garnished with chopped chives.
Note: One fresh green chilli, seeds removed and cut into fine slices, can be substituted for the chilli powder.

450 g/1 lb peeled prawns
1.2 litres/2 pints fish stock (see page 9)
1 clove garlic, crushed
a good pinch of chilli powder
1 bay leaf
juice and rind of 1 lemon
1 teaspoon ground coriander
1 teaspoon soy sauce
salt
chopped chives for garnish

SPICED CHICKEN SOUP

For 4–6 people
Preparation time 20 minutes
Cooking time approximately 1½ hours

This soup, called Soto Ajam, *is one of the few soups that does not have hot* sambal *(condiments) served with it. As with most Indonesian soups, this one tends to be more of a meat broth dish and can be served with rice as a main dish or as a light supper dish.*

1 Put the chicken, water and spring onions into a deep saucepan, add some salt and bring to the boil. Cover and simmer for 30 minutes or until the chicken is tender.
2 Remove the chicken from the pan, strain the stock and keep it aside.
3 Peel the prawns and, running a sharp knife down the backs, remove the black intestinal tracts. Chop the prawns into small pieces.
4 Heat the oil in the same pan and fry the onions and garlic until soft and golden brown.
5 Add the ground almonds, turmeric, coriander, chilli powder and ginger, fry for a few seconds, add the reserved stock and simmer for 30 minutes. Season to taste.
6 Meanwhile, remove the skin and bones from the chicken and discard.
7 Cut the meat into thin strips and put into a deep serving bowl. Add the prawns and pour the soup on top. Check the seasoning and garnish with lemon slices and parsley.

Note: To make this soup in keeping with the true Eastern style, the following garnish can be added at step 6 prior to pouring on the soup:

75 g/3 oz Chinese vermicelli, cooked and drained
50 g/2 oz celery, finely chopped
50 g/2 oz spring onions, including the green parts, chopped
2 hard-boiled eggs, peeled and coarsely chopped
3 waxy potatoes, boiled, peeled and sliced
juice of ½ lemon

1.5 kg/3 lb chicken, quartered
1.5 litres/2½ pints water
4 spring onions (optional)
salt and freshly ground black pepper
4 large Mediterranean prawns, cooked
2 tablespoons vegetable oil
110 g/4 oz onions, diced
1 clove garlic, crushed
4 whole almonds, ground, or 10 g/½ oz ground almonds
½ teaspoon turmeric
¼ teaspoon ground coriander
a pinch of chilli powder
1 teaspoon ground ginger

To garnish
2 thin slices lemon per person
a few sprigs of parsley

STARTERS

HONEYDEW MELON SALAD

For 4–8 people
Preparation time 20 minutes

1 honeydew melon
2 limes or lemons
1 tablespoon clear honey

1 Cut the melon in half and discard the seeds.
2 Scoop out the flesh with a melon baller.
3 Squeeze the juice from 1½ limes or lemons, retaining the remaining ½ lime or lemon for garnish.
4 Mix the honey into the lime or lemon juice and pour over the melon balls, mixing well to coat evenly.
5 Garnish with the remaining ½ lime or lemon cut into fine slices and serve.
Note: This is a wonderful accompaniment to a spicy main course, or as a lunchtime starter on a hot sunny day.

PRAWN AND SWEETCORN PATTIES

For 4–6 people
Preparation time 15 minutes
Cooking time 10–15 minutes

175 g/6 oz cooked prawns, shelled and finely chopped
225 g/8 oz sweetcorn kernels, canned or frozen
50 g/2 oz self-raising flour
1 teaspoon baking powder
1 egg, lightly beaten
3 tablespoons water
2 tablespoons finely chopped onion
2 cloves garlic, crushed
1 teaspoon ground coriander
½ teaspoon finely chopped celery
salt and pepper
vegetable oil for frying

This is another version of rempah *(see page 21), which has a place on any table for any occasion.*

1 Make a batter by thoroughly mixing the flour, baking powder, egg and water together.
2 Add all the other ingredients except the oil and knead the mixture well by hand, adding salt and pepper to taste.
3 Roll the mixture into balls the size of walnuts and flatten them slightly so they look like miniature burgers.
4 Heat the oil in a shallow frying pan and sauté the patties over a high heat for 2–3 minutes on both sides or until brown, or deep-fry in a pan of very hot oil.
5 Serve hot or cold as a side dish or with drinks.
Note: Traditionally, *rempah* have coconut added to them, but I think it is unnecessary in this recipe.

SPICED PRAWNS IN COCONUT MILK

For 4 people
Preparation time 30 minutes
Cooking time 15 minutes

The coconut is used here not only to add texture and flavour to the sauce, but also to bring out the flavour of the prawns.

450 g/1 lb peeled prawns, cooked
110 g/4 oz unsalted butter
110 g/4 oz onions, diced
2 teaspoons ground coriander
1 teaspoon turmeric
1 teaspoon chilli powder
½ teaspoon ground ginger
½ teaspoon salt
½ teaspoon ground black pepper
3 cloves garlic, crushed
2 tablespoons vinegar
175 ml/6 fl oz coconut milk (see page 105)
2 tablespoons tomato purée

1 Melt the butter in a heavy saucepan, add the onions and sauté gently for 5 minutes.
2 Mix the spices and seasonings with the garlic and vinegar to a smooth paste, add to the pan and cook gently, stirring continuously, for 3 minutes.
3 Pour in the coconut milk and blend into the paste, then simmer gently for 5 minutes.
4 Blend in the tomato purée, add the prawns and simmer for 2 minutes longer. Serve immediately.
Note: You may use the curry paste on page 108 in place of the garlic, spices and seasonings above. If so, sauté the onions in only half the butter.

AVOCADO WITH PRAWNS AND MANGO

For 4 people
Preparation time 20 minutes
Cooking time 15 minutes

This is my version of a prawn cocktail – interesting, exciting and imaginative. It has all the rich texture and flavour characteristic of Eastern cookery.

2 avocados
225 g/8 oz cooked and shelled prawns
225 g/8 oz mango, peeled and cubed
1 teaspoon caster sugar or to taste
110 ml/4 fl oz mayonnaise
55 ml/2 fl oz double cream
1 tablespoon finely grated horseradish
1 tablespoon lemon juice
4 slices lemon

1 Mix the prawns and mango together and sprinkle on the caster sugar. Set aside for 1 hour.
2 Combine the mayonnaise, cream, horseradish and lemon juice and mix well. Set aside for 1 hour.
3 To serve, halve the avocados, discard the stone and fill each cavity with the prawn and mango mixture. Top with the horseradish mayonnaise, garnish with a slice of lemon and serve.
Note: Cooked prawns will always benefit from a sprinkling of sugar to bring out their lovely flavour.

GINGER PRAWNS

For 4 people
Preparation time 30 minutes
Marinating time 2 hours
Cooking time 10 minutes

12 large Mediterranean prawns, precooked
55 ml/2 fl oz vegetable oil
2 tablespoons lemon juice
½ medium onion, chopped
1 heaped teaspoon diced fresh ginger
½ teaspoon chilli powder
salt and freshly ground black pepper
24 leaves fresh mint
4 sprigs fresh mint
4 lemon wedges

1 Peel the prawns, leaving the tail tips on. Run a sharp knife down the back of the prawns and remove the dark digestive tracts.
2 Put 2 tablespoons of the oil into a blender and add the lemon juice, onion, ginger, chilli, salt and black pepper and purée to a smooth paste.
3 Place the prawns on a shallow tray, pour the paste over them and leave to marinate for at least 2 hours.
4 Wrap each prawn in 2 mint leaves, then thread the prawns onto very fine individual skewers.
5 Preheat the grill to high and heat the prawns, brushing regularly with the remaining oil, until they are hot.
6 Serve immediately, garnished with mint and lemon wedges.

Note: Most large Mediterranean prawns are sold precooked and frozen and there are roughly 25 to 1 kg/2 lb. If you are lucky enough to obtain fresh prawns (that is, uncooked), then the recipe above will still apply except that the cooking time will take a little longer – approximately 10 –15 minutes.

Instead of the chilli powder, try using 1 fresh, hot green chilli.

FRIED SPICED PRAWNS

For 4 people
Preparation time 20 minutes
Cooking time 15 minutes

In Asia the Green Tiger prawn is generally used for this dish. A similar variety of prawn is available in Australia and North America, but in England Mediterranean prawns are an excellent alternative. These are generally sold precooked and frozen.

12–16 Mediterranean prawns (not less than 7.5 cm/ 3 inches long)
salt
50 g/2 oz flour
½ teaspoon ground coriander
1 teaspoon chilli powder
1 egg, beaten with a little milk
110 g/4 oz breadcrumbs
175 ml/6 fl oz vegetable oil

1 If frozen, make sure the prawns are totally defrosted. Remove the heads, peel the body, leaving the tail fins on.
2 Run a sharp knife down the back to expose the digestive tract and remove. Season with salt.
3 Mix the flour, ground coriander and chilli powder together, then pass through a fine sieve.
4 Dust the prawns liberally with the spiced flour, dip each into the beaten egg and milk mixture, then coat in breadcrumbs.
5 When all the prawns are done, heat the oil in a deep frying pan and cook the prawns a few at a time until crisp and golden.

CHILLI PRAWNS

For 4 people
Preparation time 30 minutes
Cooking time 10 minutes

450 g/1 lb peeled prawns, cooked
55 ml/2 fl oz vegetable oil
50 g/2 oz onions, diced
1 clove garlic, crushed
2 red chillies, seeds removed and sliced
½ teaspoon ground ginger
1 small green pepper, seeds and pith removed and sliced
1 tablespoon chilli sauce (see note)
1 tablespoon tomato purée
salt and pepper
1 teaspoon caster sugar
4 spring onions

1 Heat the oil in a large, deep frying pan and sauté the onions gently for 2 minutes. Add the garlic, chillies, ginger and green pepper and continue to cook for 3 minutes more.

2 Stir in the chilli sauce and tomato purée and sauté for a further 2 minutes.

3 Add the shelled prawns and sauté for 1 minute or until heated through and well coated with the sauce. Season to taste with salt and pepper and sprinkle on the caster sugar.

4 Transfer to a warm serving dish and garnish with the chopped spring onions. Serve immediately.

Note: Most shops these days sell countless varieties of chilli sauce but make sure you get the Chinese variety for this recipe as it tends to be not too hot and is also slightly sweet.

SPICED CRAB CLAWS

For 4 people
Preparation time 20 minutes
Cooking time 10 minutes

8 large crab claws
5 tablespoons vegetable oil
110 g/4 oz onions, diced
2 cloves garlic, crushed
1 teaspoon chilli powder
1 teaspoon ground ginger
½ teaspoon ground coriander
3 tablespoons water
2 teaspoons soy sauce
1 teaspoon brown sugar
2 teaspoons tomato purée
salt
Juice of ½ lemon

Crab claws are generally available already cleaned, boiled and frozen. This recipe is designed specifically for crab claws so, if you happen to have whole crabs, keep the bodies for another recipe.

1 Fry the crab claws in hot oil for 5 minutes. Drain and put them in a warm oven.

2 Fry the onions and garlic in the same pan for 2 minutes. Add the chilli powder, ginger and coriander, then add the water, soy sauce, sugar, tomato purée and a little salt.

3 Simmer for 2 or 3 minutes, put in the crab claws, add the lemon juice and stir to coat the crab claws. Serve hot.

Note: If you can replace the chilli powder with 6 red chillies, deseeded and diced, the flavour will be much better.

JAVANESE OMELETTE

For 2 people
Preparation time 10 minutes
Cooking time 10 minutes

I first came across this omelette at a breakfast table with a friend in Java. I will leave it to you to decide what kind of effect it had on me at the time.

4 eggs
1 tablespoon water
salt
2 teaspoons soy sauce
1 teaspoon brown sugar
2 tablespoons vegetable oil
50 g/2 oz onions, finely diced
½ teaspoon chilli powder
1 teaspoon paprika

1 Beat the eggs lightly, adding the water and a little salt halfway through.
2 Mix the soy sauce and brown sugar together until the sugar dissolves and then add to the egg.
3 Heat the oil in a pan, fry the onions until soft, add the chilli powder and paprika and stir in well.
4 Add the egg and soy sauce mixture and allow to half set, stirring a little so that any remaining liquid comes into contact with the pan.
5 Fry until golden brown on the bottom, then place the pan under a hot grill to finish off the top. The idea is to leave the omelette in one unbroken piece. Transfer to a plate and serve.
Note: For the authentic flavour, add 2 red chillies, deseeded and diced, to the onions at step 3, leaving out the chilli powder and paprika.

STEAMED EGG ROLLS

For 6 people
Preparation time 30 minutes
Cooking time 20 minutes

For the egg wrapper
6 eggs, lightly beaten
a little oil for greasing

For the filling
225 g/8 oz minced lean beef
a good pinch of ground ginger
1 teaspoon soy sauce
2 teaspoons cornflour
salt and freshly ground pepper
30 ml/1 fl oz vegetable oil
25 g/1 oz onions, finely diced
25 g/1 oz celery, finely diced
50 g/2 oz carrots, grated
4 spring onions, finely diced
a pinch of cayenne pepper

1 Grease a shallow frying pan, put over a high heat and make 6 very thin omelettes, one at a time. As they are cooked, pile them on top of each other on the back of a plate, separating each omelette with a sheet of greaseproof paper.
2 Mix the minced meat with the ginger, soy sauce and cornflour and season with a little salt and pepper.
3 Heat the oil in a frying pan and sauté the onions until soft. Add the celery, carrots and meat and stir until the meat changes colour.
4 Put in the spring onions and cayenne pepper. Stir once more and remove from the heat. Divide into six portions and set aside to cool.
5 When the filling is cool, place each portion in the middle of an omelette, bringing the two edges towards the middle and then rolling the bottom upwards. Make sure that the filling is completely enclosed. Seal each roll with paste, made by mixing a little flour and water.
6 Steam on a rack over boiling water in a covered pan for a few minutes until hot. Serve with a salad.

Spiced Meat Soup (see page 12), *Sour Prawn Soup* (see page 12) *and Chilled Coconut Soup* (see page 11)

SPICED SCRAMBLED EGGS

For 4 people
Preparation time 15 minutes
Cooking time 15 minutes

This is a wonderful way to start a Sunday morning breakfast . . . or perhaps a starter for a dinner party.

8 eggs
4 tomatoes, skinned, deseeded and chopped
1 teaspoon salt
50 g/2 oz unsalted butter
110 g/4 oz onions, diced
2 green chillies, deseeded and finely sliced
1 teaspoon turmeric
1 teaspoon ground coriander

1 Place the eggs, tomatoes and salt in a deep bowl and beat well.
2 Heat the butter in a frying pan and sauté the onions gently for 5 minutes.
3 Add the chillies and spices and fry gently for 2 minutes, stirring constantly.
4 Pour in the beaten egg mixture and stir gently with a large wooden spoon until the eggs are scrambled. Serve immediately with buttered toast.
Note: Chilli powder is not a good substitute for fresh green chillies in this particular dish.

SAVOURY POTATO ROLLS

For 4–6 people
Preparation time 20 minutes
Cooking time 30 minutes

For the jacket
50 g/2 oz butter
225 ml/8 fl oz water
110 g/4 oz plain flour
1 teaspoon salt
1 egg
225 g/8 oz potatoes, peeled, boiled and mashed

For the filling
175 g/6 oz minced lean beef
1 teaspoon soy sauce
½ teaspoon sugar
1 teaspoon ground coriander
salt and freshly ground pepper
2 tablespoons vegetable oil
110 g/4 oz onions, diced
2 cloves garlic, crushed
1 egg, beaten
breadcrumbs for coating
oil for deep-frying

1 To make the jacket, boil the butter and water together in a saucepan. Sift the flour and salt into the mixture and beat well. Continue cooking and beating the mixture until it begins to leave the sides of the pan. Remove from the heat and gradually beat in the egg. When this is totally incorporated, add the mashed potato and mix well until finely blended. Set aside.
2 Mix the meat with the soy sauce, sugar, coriander and a little salt and pepper to taste.
3 Heat the oil in a shallow frying pan and fry the onions until soft, about 2–3 minutes. Put in the garlic and stir well.
4 Add the seasoned meat and stir-fry until it changes colour and is cooked, about 10 minutes. Remove from the pan and set aside to cool.
5 Take a large tablespoon of the potato mixture in your hands and mould it into a flat round. Place a little cooked filling in the middle and fold and roll to mould into balls.
6 Dip each roll into beaten egg, coat with breadcrumbs and deep-fry in plenty of hot oil until golden brown. Remove from the oil and drain on kitchen paper towel. Serve at once.
Note: Minced chicken breast or pork may be used instead of beef.

SPICED POTATO PATTIES

For 4 people
Preparation time 1 hour
Cooking time 30 minutes

1 kg/2 lb potatoes, peeled
1 teaspoon salt
2 tablespoons finely chopped mint leaves
2 spring onions, finely chopped
1 fresh green chilli, deseeded and finely chopped
1 egg, beaten
breadcrumbs for coating
oil for deep-frying

For the filling
25 g/1 oz unsalted butter
225 g/8 oz onions, finely diced
1 clove garlic
1 teaspoon chopped fresh ginger
2 teaspoons curry powder
½ teaspoon salt
1 tablespoon lemon juice
225 g/8 oz minced beef or lamb
150 ml/¼ pint water
1 teaspoon mixed spices (see page 106)
2 tablespoons chopped parsley

1 To make the filling, heat the butter in a saucepan and sauté half the onions for 3 minutes. Add the garlic and ginger and cook for a further 2 minutes.
2 Add the curry powder, salt and lemon juice and mix well. Cook for another minute, then add the minced beef or lamb and continue cooking over a high heat, stirring continuously, until all the meat changes colour.
3 Turn the heat down and add the water. Continue to cook until all the liquid evaporates and the mince is tender. As the liquid evaporates, stir continuously to prevent the meat from sticking to the pan.
4 Sprinkle with mixed spices and chopped parsley, remove from the heat, stir well and set aside to cool. Mix in the reserved chopped onion.
5 To make the patties, boil and mash the potatoes smoothly. Blend in the salt, mint, spring onions and chilli.
6 Divide into eight portions and shape each into a ball, then press them flat.
7 Put a spoonful of the meat filling in the centre and close the potato around it, shaping it into a thick round patty.
8 Dip in beaten egg then in the breadcrumbs and fry in hot oil for 3 minutes one side, turn over and fry for 2 minutes the other side or until golden brown. Serve immediately.
Note: Leeks may be used in place of the spring onions, and a pinch of chilli powder can be substituted for the fresh chillies in the potato mixture. Fresh mint, finely chopped, will give extra flavour if added to the meat at step 3.

MEAT AND COCONUT PATTIES

For 4–6 people
Preparation time 20 minutes
Cooking time 20 minutes

These patties are known as rempah *and are the Eastern equivalent of the Western hamburger. They are just as easy to make and are usually eaten as a snack or hors d'oeuvre, but can be an excellent main dish served with a rice or noodle dish and some vegetables.*

450 g/1 lb minced lean beef
175 g/6 oz desiccated coconut
150 ml/¼ pint milk
2 cloves garlic, crushed
1 teaspoon ground coriander
½ teaspoon ground cumin
2 eggs, lightly beaten
salt
55 ml/2 fl oz vegetable oil

1 Moisten the coconut with the milk and set aside for 10 minutes.
2 Mix the beef, garlic, coriander, cumin, eggs, moistened coconut and salt to taste together in a deep bowl. Shape into patties.
3 Heat the oil in a frying pan until very hot to seal the patties, then sauté the patties gently on a low heat for 5 minutes on one side. Turn over and cook for 3 minutes on the other side.
4 Serve as a starter with a salad or as a main course with Yellow Rice (see page 94).
Note: If this is being made as a main dish, just double the quantities.

GALLOPING HORSES

For 8 people
Preparation time 15 minutes
Cooking time 20 minutes

This rather exotically named dish is the Asian version of Angels on Horseback. Traditionally Thai in origin, it is used extensively in Java as an hors d'oeuvre and has that unusual combination of sweet and savoury.

350 g/12 oz minced pork
30 ml/1 fl oz peanut or vegetable oil
110 g/4 oz onions, finely diced
1 clove garlic, crushed
50 g/2 oz roasted peanuts, ground, or 1 tablespoon peanut butter
50 g/2 oz brown sugar
salt and freshly ground black pepper
1 fresh pineapple, peeled, cored and sliced into rounds
a little cayenne pepper
2 tablespoons chopped parsley

1 Heat the oil and sauté the onions in a large frying pan over a medium heat for 5 minutes or until the onions are soft. Add the crushed garlic and cook a minute longer.
2 Stir in the minced pork and fry gently until it changes colour.
3 Add the peanuts, sugar and a little salt and pepper to taste. Reduce the heat and cook gently for 10 minutes or until the pork is cooked and the mixture is fairly dry. Remove from the heat.
4 Sprinkle a little ground black pepper on each pineapple ring and carefully spoon enough of the pork mixture on top to form and shape little mounds. Add a tiny pinch of cayenne pepper to each, then place on a large serving dish.
5 Scatter the chopped parsley over and serve immediately.
Note: A whole dried chilli, crumbled, may be substituted for the cayenne, but be careful as it may be a little too hot for some tastes. If available, coriander should be used in place of parsley.

Steamed Egg Rolls (see page 19), *Avocado with Prawns and Mango* (see page 15) *and Chilli Prawns* (see page 17)

Fish and Shellfish

All the lands of Southeast Asia at some point have access to the sea and therefore have a great range of seafood at their disposal. In some areas, fish does not play a major role on the daily menu and is sometimes considered to be inferior food. Whether it is considered a superior or inferior food source, one thing is certain: Asians are experts at preparing and cooking fish. As in most culinary-orientated societies, great attention is always paid to the seasons and the availability of the right fish at the right time. What cooks best and in what manner? Is it better sautéed? Should it be steamed or stir-fried? Is it better curried or devilled? and the deliberation goes on. Mackerel sautées beautifully but steams badly; sea bass, turbot, halibut and brill are delicious steamed; pike poaches well. Fish-based stocks and soups are an intrinsic part of culinary life, especially in Indonesia, Burma and Thailand. Many of the basic cooking methods are generally handed down by word of mouth from generation to generation to exist inseparably with regional folklore.

It is not essential, but it is a good idea to learn a little about the nature of presenting fish at the table. As in the Yin and Yang of the Chinese, there are always opposites. Some fish are considered to be of the 'cooling' variety and therefore should be accompanied by hot or spicy sauces, relishes or vegetables. Crabs, lobsters, oysters and scallops are considered 'hot' foods, like garlic, which arouse the desires and passions of the body, and should therefore be tempered with limes and lemon, lettuce, cucumber and milk, which are considered 'cooling'. It is always wise to follow one with the other to give a balanced meal. Once you have become acquainted with the basic rules regarding the combination of ingredients and adhered to the rules of health and hygiene, the rest is open to skill and imagination – an Aladdin's cave of culinary treasure!

MALACCAN FISH

For 4 people
Preparation time 20 minutes
Marinating time 30 minutes
Cooking time 20 minutes

700 g/1½ lb cod fillets, skinned and cut into 4
3 medium onions, finely chopped
2 cloves garlic, crushed
a pinch of chilli powder or cayenne pepper
½ teaspoon dried basil
½ teaspoon fresh ginger, crushed, or ¼ teaspoon ground ginger
4 anchovy fillets
1 tablespoon ground almonds
juice of ½ lemon
225 ml/8 fl oz thick coconut milk (see page 105)
4 lemon or lime wedges

1 Place the onions, garlic, chilli powder or cayenne, dried basil, ginger, anchovies, ground almonds, lemon juice and coconut milk in a blender or food processor and blend well.
2 Place the fish in a flat container and pour over the blended ingredients and marinate for 30 minutes.
3 Meanwhile, heat the grill to medium high. Remove the fillets from the marinade and grill for 10–15 minutes, basting with the marinade as they cook. When cooked, set aside in a warm place.
4 Pour the remaining marinade into a small pan, bring to the boil and simmer until the marinade thickens. Strain.
5 To serve, pour the sauce onto hot plates. Place the fish on top and garnish with lemon or lime wedges.
Note: If you wish a stronger flavour, increase the chilli powder and garlic as much as required.

SPICED PLAICE

For 4 people
Preparation time 10 minutes
Marinating time 1 hour
Cooking time 10–15 minutes

This mild, soft-fleshed fish, which is the mainstay of every fish and chip shop in England, has been given the Indonesian (with Chinese and Malay influence) treatment.

4 plaice, cleaned, gutted and dark skin removed
150 ml/¼ pint soy sauce
25 g/1 oz soft brown sugar
½ teaspoon chilli powder
2 cloves garlic, crushed
50 g/2 oz butter
juice of 1 lemon

1 Combine the soy sauce, sugar, chilli and garlic and stir until the sugar dissolves.
2 Lay the fish in a shallow dish and pour over the soy sauce mixture, brushing the fish well to work in the marinade. Cover and set aside for 1 hour, basting occasionally.
3 Preheat the grill to high. Arrange the fish on the rack of the grill and cook the fish for approximately 6 minutes on one side and 4 minutes on the other, basting with the marinating liquor.
4 Melt the butter in a small pan, add the lemon juice, stir well and remove from the heat. Discard the remaining marinade.
5 Transfer the fish to individual plates, pour on the butter and lemon mixture and serve at once.

JAVANESE GRILLED FISH

For 2 people
Preparation time 15 minutes
Marinating time 25 minutes
Cooking time 25 minutes

The original recipe called for a large sea bream. As these are not common in fishmongers in England, I have substituted plaice.

1 large plaice, cleaned, scaled and black skin removed
1 tablespoon brown sugar
2 tablespoons soy sauce
1 clove garlic, crushed
50 g/2 oz onions, finely diced
1 tablespoon water
salt
10 g/½ oz unsalted butter
½ teaspoon chilli powder
juice of ½ lemon

1 Put the plaice in a large shallow dish.
2 Dissolve the sugar in the soy sauce.
3 Mix the crushed garlic and onions with 1 tablespoon of the soy sauce and dilute with the water.
4 Pour this over the fish, making sure you rub the marinade well in, sprinkle with a little salt and set aside for 1 hour.
5 Preheat the grill on a low setting, remove the fish from the marinade and place under the grill.
6 Add the rest of the soy sauce to the marinade and baste the fish as it cooks.
7 Cook for 15 minutes. Carefully turn the fish over and cook for a further 10 minutes.
8 Lay the fish on a serving plate, melt the butter, add the remaining marinade, chilli powder and lemon juice, mix well and pour over the fish. Serve immediately.
Note: If you want a truly authentic Javanese grilled fish, you must get a sea bream, have it scaled and cleaned, then follow the above recipe but cook it over a low charcoal fire. It is well worth the extra effort. Replace the chilli powder with 4 red chillies, deseeded and finely diced.

MACKEREL PALLU MARA

For 4 people
Preparation time 15 minutes
Cooking time 50 minutes

Pallu Mara *means food poached until dry – in this case, mackerel. The taut, mottled, steel-blue skin covers pink-tinted flesh, which is firm, richly flavoured, oily and rich in vitamins. This fish is ideal for this dish, which is always served cold.*

Meat and Coconut Patties (see page 21), *Spiced Crab Claws* (see page 17) *and Savoury Potato Rolls* (see page 20)

4 mackerel, weighing approximately 450 g/1 lb each
1 teaspoon turmeric
salt
3 cloves garlic, crushed
1 large onion, diced
1 large red pepper, deseeded and cut into fine strips
1 tablespoon brown sugar
350 ml/12 fl oz white wine vinegar
1 teaspoon ground ginger

1 Clean the mackerel, then rub the turmeric and a little salt in to them.
2 Spread half the garlic, half the onion and half the red pepper on the bottom of a pan large enough to hold all the fish.
3 Lay the fish on top and place the remainder of the garlic, onion and pepper over the fish.
4 Dissolve the sugar in the wine vinegar, mix in the ground ginger and pour this over the fish adding a sprinkle of salt.
5 Cover the pan and cook slowly over a low heat for 50 minutes, gently shaking the pan from time to time so the fish will not stick or burn.
6 Remove from the heat and set aside until cold. This should ideally be served the following day without the onion mixture, which is for flavouring only.
Note: The traditional way of cooking this dish is to use 10 red chillies, deseeded and sliced, instead of the red pepper. Tamarind water is also used in place of the wine vinegar. Understandably, if you follow tradition, the flavour will change slightly but, whichever recipe you use, the unique flavour of this dish will leave you with thoughts of the East.

YELLOW MACKEREL

For 4 people
Preparation time 20 minutes
Marinating time 1 hour
Cooking time 10 minutes

4 × 450 g/1 lb mackerel, filleted
275 ml/½ pint lime or lemon juice
1 teaspoon grated lime or lemon rind
50 g/2 oz onions, finely diced
55 ml/2 fl oz white wine vinegar
1 teaspoon salt
1 teaspoon coarsely ground black pepper
1 teaspoon turmeric
55 ml/2 fl oz vegetable oil

1 Mix together the lime or lemon juice and rind, onions, wine vinegar, ½ teaspoon salt and the black pepper in a shallow dish.
2 Lay the fish in the dish and baste well. Set aside for 1 hour, basting occasionally.
3 Remove from the marinade, pat dry with paper towel. Rub the fish all over with the remaining salt and turmeric.
4 Strain the marinade through a fine sieve and reserve about 150 ml/¼ pint.
5 Heat the oil in a large frying pan and sauté the fish for about 5 minutes on each side.
6 Remove from the pan and pat dry with paper towel. Transfer to a warm serving dish. Serve the reserved marinade separately.

MARINATED FISH

For 6 people
Preparation time 15 minutes
Marinating time 24 hours

Anton Mosimann of the Dorchester Hotel, London taught me the value of being able to make food taste of 'what it is'. I will always remember the look of complete joy on his face the day he showed me some beautiful Scottish salmon fillets he was marinating in oil, dill, peppercorns, sugar and slices of orange and lemon. That man breathes poetry into food with the simplest of ideas and I humbly dedicate this dish to him as a token of my thanks for the inspiration he has given me.

6 whiting fillets
3 tablespoons fresh lime juice
2 tablespoons light soy sauce
75 ml/3 fl oz coconut milk (see page 105)
1 fresh green chilli
2 spring onions
fresh, crisp lettuce leaves

1 Cut the fish fillets into thin strips and place in a bowl.
2 Cover with the mixture of lime juice, soy sauce and coconut milk. Cover with plastic cling film and store in the refrigerator for 24 hours, brushing the fish pieces from time to time with the marinade juices.
3 Remove the seeds from the chilli and finely dice the chilli and the spring onions.
4 Line a serving dish or individual plates with lettuce leaves. Lay the fish pieces on top, sprinkle the finely diced spring onions and chilli over them, pour on the marinade and serve.
Note: Slices of fresh lime may accompany this dish, and it may be served as a starter with avocado or in a glass with shredded lettuce. However, I prefer it as a main course with various salads and rice dishes.

SWEET AND SOUR FISH

For 4 people
Preparation time 10 minutes
Cooking time 25 minutes

The original Malaysian name for this dish is Ikan Cuka *which, translated literally, is, 'Vinegar Fish'; this makes it seem a rather unappetizing dish, which it certainly is not.*

450 g/1 lb halibut fillets, skinned
110 g/4 oz onions, diced
½ clove garlic, crushed
¼ teaspoon ground ginger
1 teaspoon ground almonds
¼ teaspoon chilli powder
55 ml/2 fl oz vegetable oil
150 ml/¼ pint water
30 ml/1 fl oz wine vinegar
½ teaspoon soft brown sugar
salt and freshly ground pepper

1 Preheat the oven to 180°C/350°F/Gas Mark 4.
2 Put the onions, garlic, ginger, almonds, chilli powder and oil into a blender and purée until smooth.
3 Pour this mixture into a frying pan and sauté gently for 2 or 3 minutes. Do not allow to burn.
4 Add the water, wine vinegar and sugar. Bring to the boil, turn down the heat and simmer gently for 5 minutes.
5 Pour this into a casserole dish or baking tin large enough to lay the

fish out flat without overlapping. Put in the fish, season with a little salt and pepper, cover with a lid or foil and put into the oven for 15 minutes.
6 Serve in the casserole dish or transfer to a warm serving plate.
Note: Brazil nuts may replace the almonds. A teaspoon of commercial chilli paste can be used instead of chilli powder and a piece of fresh ginger in place of the ground ginger.

HALIBUT WITH CRAB SAUCE

For 4–6 people
Preparation time 30 minutes
Cooking time 15 minutes

1 kg/2 lb halibut or other white fish fillets, skin removed
2 pinches ground ginger
1 teaspoon salt
2 teaspoons cornflour
oil for deep-frying

Sauce
2 tablespoons vegetable oil
3 shallots or 6 spring onions
a good pinch of ground ginger
150 ml/¼ pint fish stock
175 g/6 oz crab meat, cooked
freshly ground white pepper
2 teaspoons cornflour mixed with a little cold water
salt (optional)

This most interesting style of food is peculiar to Singapore and is known as Nonya. *It is a mixture of Chinese and Indonesian ingredients and cooked in a way that is reminiscent of what the East is best known for – the integration and mingling of cultures.* Nonya *recipes are usually hot and spicy, based primarily on a* sambal *– a paste of various spices, chillies and onions, etc.*

1 To make the sauce, heat the oil and gently sauté the shallots for 1 minute – if using spring onions, then sauté for only a few seconds. Add ginger and stock, stir and simmer for 2–3 minutes.
2 Add the crab meat, heat through for no longer than a minute and season with pepper.
3 Stir in the cornflour mixture and keep stirring until it boils. Reduce the heat to low and simmer gently for 5 minutes. Add a little salt if required.
4 Cut the fillets into bite-size pieces and put into a bowl. Sprinkle on the ginger, salt and cornflour. Toss well to coat all the pieces.
5 Heat the oil in a deep pan and quickly fry the fish a few pieces at a time for 1 minute over a medium heat. Drain on absorbent paper towel and keep warm while cooking the remainder.
6 Arrange the fish on a serving dish, pour the sauce over and serve immediately.

Halibut with Crab Sauce, Lobster and Courgette Curry (see page 36) *with Indonesian Pancakes* (see page 102) *and Special Spiced Rice* (see page 96)

HALIBUT WITH PINEAPPLE CREAM AND CARAMEL

For 4 people
Preparation time 30 minutes
Cooking time 20 minutes

Southeast Asia, with its sophisticated and highly complex culture, has overtones of Chinese, Indian and French influences in its cuisine that make it unique. Even though I have 'Westernized' this recipe slightly, it still has that distinct combination of flavours.

4 × 225 g/8 oz halibut fillets
150 g/5 oz fresh pineapple, finely diced
25 g/1 oz butter
25 g/1 oz shallots, peeled and finely diced
salt and freshly ground pepper
55 ml/2 fl oz white wine
2 anchovy fillets
150 ml/¼ pint fish stock (see page 9)
75 ml/3 fl oz double cream
1 tablespoon caramelized sugar (see recipe below)
a pinch of caster sugar

1 Blanch the pineapple in boiling water for 1 minute, then remove and plunge immediately into cold water. Set aside.
2 Grease a casserole dish well with the butter and sprinkle in the shallots.
3 Season the halibut fillets generously and place them in the casserole dish together with the wine.
4 Purée the anchovy fillets in a liquidizer with the fish stock and pour into the dish.
5 Cover and poach in a preheated 190°C/375°F/Gas Mark 5 oven for 8–12 minutes.
6 Remove from the oven and keep the halibut fillets covered and in a warm place.
7 Strain the stock into a pan, add the pineapple and reduce the stock by half.
8 Add the cream and reduce the sauce by half again.
9 Add the caramelized sugar and blend well.
10 Place the halibut fillets on warm plates. Season the sauce with salt and pepper and good pinch of sugar and cover each fillet with the sauce. Serve immediately.

CARAMELIZED SUGAR

50 g/2 oz caster sugar
175 ml/6 fl oz water
juice of ½ lemon

1 Melt the sugar in 110 ml/4 fl oz of water in a small pan over a gentle heat.
2 When melted, turn the heat to high and cook the syrup until dark brown, stirring constantly.
3 Still stirring, add the rest of the water and blend in.
4 Continue cooking over high heat for 2 minutes, then add the lemon juice.
5 Blend well, remove from the heat and leave to cool.

STEAMED FISH WITH COCONUT AND SESAME

For 6 people
Preparation time 30 minutes
Cooking time 20 minutes

1 Rinse the fish fillets in cold water and pat dry with absorbent towel.
2 Put the desiccated coconut, hot milk, garlic and fresh ginger into a blender and blend until the coconut becomes finely ground. Transfer to a bowl.
3 Add the sesame seeds, salt, turmeric, pepper, lemon juice, flour and chopped parsley and mix well.
4 Cut the fish into serving pieces.
5 Cut the foil into six squares large enough to completely cover and seal the fish pieces.
6 Lay the pieces of fish on the foil squares, cover each with some of the coconut mixture, then fold the foil over and seal the edges.
7 Steam the fish pieces over hot water for 20 minutes in the oven set at 190°C/375°F/Gas Mark 5, or for 15 minutes over hot water on top of the cooker. Serve in the parcels.

1 kg/2 lb fish fillets (any white fish)
75 g/3 oz desiccated coconut
110 ml/4 fl oz hot milk
1 clove garlic, crushed
1 tablespoon grated fresh ginger
2 tablespoons toasted sesame seeds
1 teaspoon salt
1 teaspoon turmeric
1 teaspoon ground black pepper
juice of ½ lemon
2 tablespoons rice flour
2 tablespoons chopped parsley

FISH CURRY

For 4 people
Preparation time 20 minutes
Cooking time 30 minutes

Asian curries are a far cry from the Indian curries that we know in Europe. Here is a typical example.

1 Heat 1 tablespoon oil in a pan and quickly sauté the fish on both sides. Remove from the heat and set aside.
2 Meanwhile, heat the remaining oil in another pan and fry the garlic and onions until tender.
3 Quickly stir in the coriander, lemon rind, chilli powder, turmeric, a little salt and the cooking apple. Let this cook slowly on a low heat for 10 minutes, without burning.
4 Add the fish and all the juices from the pan, cover and simmer for a further 5 minutes.
5 Add the coconut milk and cook gently for 5 more minutes.
6 Serve hot garnished with sliced cucumber and chopped mint.
Note: Monkfish or scampi can be used in place of haddock, but they do not need to be cooked separately.

700 g/1½ lb haddock fillets, cut into small cubes
2 tablespoons vegetable oil
2 cloves garlic
175 g/6 oz onions, finely diced
2 teaspoons ground coriander
grated rind of 1 lemon
1 teaspoon chilli powder
1 teaspoon turmeric
salt
1 tart cooking apple, peeled, cored and diced
225 ml/8 fl oz thick coconut milk (see page 105)
sliced cucumber and chopped mint to garnish

SUNSET FISH

For 4 people
Preparation time 25 minutes
Cooking time 30 minutes

450 g/1 lb whiting, cod or halibut or other firm white fish fillets, skinned
55 ml/2 fl oz vegetable oil
175 g/6 oz onions, diced
2 cloves garlic, crushed
1 red chilli, chopped (optional)
6 tomatoes, skinned, deseeded and chopped
1 tablespoon tomato purée
55 ml/2 fl oz water
30 ml/1 fl oz wine vinegar
salt and freshly ground pepper
1 tablespoon chopped parsley
4 spring onions

This is so called because of the brilliant colours of the dish when served. I believe it is traditionally a Thai dish, although its origins are a little obscure. Don't you think it is slightly reminiscent of Italian cuisine?

1 Heat the oil in a large, deep frying pan and, when hot, sauté the onions for 3 minutes. Add the garlic and chilli, if used.
2 Add the tomatoes, tomato purée, water and vinegar, bring to the boil and simmer, covered, for 10 minutes.
3 Season the fish fillets with salt and pepper, place in the sauce and baste liberally. Re-cover the pan and simmer for 15 minutes.
4 Just before serving add the parsley, stir in, then transfer to a warm serving dish. Sprinkle over the spring onions and serve.
Note: You may wish to use a 400 g/14 oz can of tomatoes in place of the fresh tomatoes; if so, omit the water. A pinch of cayenne pepper or chilli powder would go well in place of the fresh red chilli.

SPICED FISH STEAKS

For 4 people
Preparation time 20 minutes
Marinating time 30 minutes
Cooking time 45 minutes

4 fish steaks or fillets, weighing approximately 175 g/6 oz each
3 teaspoons lemon juice
1 teaspoon turmeric
salt
110 g/4 oz butter
175 g/6 oz onions, diced
25 g/1 oz garlic, crushed
1 teaspoon ground ginger
2 teaspoons ground coriander
2 teaspoons ground cumin
2 teaspoons ground fenugreek
1 teaspoon caster sugar
275 ml/½ pint yoghurt
½ teaspoon garam masala
1 tablespoon parsley

This is a spicy way to cook fish, but the steaks must be compact, in other words firm-fleshed, such as tuna or other fish of that family, angler-fish, swordfish, shark or dogfish. These are not common in every country so I have adjusted this recipe for halibut or turbot.

1 Mix together the lemon juice and turmeric and brush over the fillets, coating well. Sprinkle with a little salt and marinate for 30 minutes.
2 Heat the butter in a frying pan large enough to hold the fish pieces and fry them on a medium heat for about 5 minutes, turning them over once. Remove from the pan and keep warm in the oven.
3 Sauté the onions and garlic in the same pan on a low heat for about 10 minutes, adding the ginger halfway through.
4 Remove the frying pan from the heat, add the coriander, cumin, fenugreek, 1 teaspoon salt, the sugar and yoghurt. Mix well and return the pan to the low heat.
5 Add the fish pieces, cover and simmer still on the low heat for 15

minutes, stirring occasionally to prevent the sauce sticking.

6 Just before serving, sprinkle on the garam masala and chopped parsley and simmer for another 2–3 minutes.

Note: If the sauce becomes a little too dry for your liking, a little water may be added at step 6. A little more 'spice' may be added to this dish by slitting 2 green chillies lengthways, removing all the seeds, chopping the flesh into fine slices and adding to the dish at step 6.

FISH ROLLS WITH SATAY SAUCE

For 2–4 people
Preparation time 1 hour
Cooking time 25 minutes

These fish rolls have all the appearances of a Chinese dish, but are served with a Malay sauce; this typifies the integration of cuisines in Indonesia.

450 g/1 lb cod or haddock fillets
110 g/4 oz onions, diced
3 cloves garlic
1 egg
1 tablespoon plain flour
2 teaspoons chopped parsley
salt and pepper
75 g/3 oz fresh breadcrumbs
oil for deep-frying

Satay sauce
2 tablespoons peanut or vegetable oil
50 g/2 oz onions, finely diced
1 clove garlic, crushed
2 teaspoons ground coriander
1 teaspoon ground fennel
1 teaspoon ground cumin
½ teaspoon ground chilli
75 g/3 oz peanuts, roasted and roughly ground
150 ml/½ pint coconut milk (see page 105)
4 tablespoons white wine vinegar
1 teaspoon brown sugar
juice of ½ lemon
salt

1 For the *Satay* sauce, heat the oil in a saucepan and gently fry the onions and garlic for 2–3 minutes.

2 Add all the dry spices and cook for another minute, stirring continuously.

3 Put in the ground peanuts, coconut milk, wine vinegar and sugar and stir well. Bring to the boil and simmer gently for 10 minutes.

4 For the fish rolls, put the fish fillets into a blender or food processor and blend to a smooth paste.

5 Add the onions and garlic and blend again to incorporate these into the paste.

6 Put in the egg, flour and chopped parsley and season well with salt and pepper. Blend again for 10 seconds.

7 Put the fish paste from the blender into a bowl and chill in the freezer for 15 minutes.

8 Shape into rolls about 7.5 cm/3 inches long and 2.5 cm/1 inch thick and coat generously in breadcrumbs.

9 Deep-fry in hot oil until golden brown, about 2–3 minutes. Lift from oil and drain on absorbent paper.

10 Arrange the fish rolls on warm plates. Add the lemon juice to the sauce and season to taste. Stir well, then pour into a sauceboat or individual ramekins and serve immediately.

Note: The dry spices will have a better and more aromatic flavour if they are bought whole and ground before use. The easiest way of doing this is in a coffee grinder, but the more traditional way is with a pestle and mortar.

LOBSTER AND COURGETTE CURRY

For 2 people
Preparation time 1½ hours
Cooking time 20 minutes

This recipe is slightly complicated, but if you read the instructions carefully before you start and then read them again, you will understand it and the finished result will be well worth the extra effort.

2 small lobsters (just over 450 g/1 lb each), cooked
225 g/8 oz courgettes, cut into quarters lengthways and diced
25 g/1 oz butter
110 g/4 oz onions, finely diced
2 fresh red chillies, deseeded and finely sliced
1 teaspoon grated lemon rind
1 teaspoon turmeric
½ teaspoon dried basil
75 ml/3 fl oz water
275 ml/½ pint coconut milk (see page 105)
salt and freshly ground pepper
juice of ½ lemon

1 Remove the claws from the lobsters. Bend the smaller, movable pincer backwards until it comes away and a piece of the cartilage will come with it. Crack the shell of the claw at the thickest part with the flat of a heavy knife or a meat bat, without crushing it, and you should be able to pull out the claw meat in one piece. Repeat with the smaller pincer. Put the flesh on one side and keep the pieces of shell.
2 Extract the flesh from the tail by rotating it in the opposite direction to the head and pulling apart. Cut through the underside of the tail with a strong pair of kitchen scissors. Pull this away from the tail to expose the flesh and then ease the flesh away from the protective outer shell.
3 Remove the legs, including the sections joining them to the underside of the head. Put 8 legs and 1 head on one side on a plate.
4 You should now have a plate with the flesh of the tail and claws, a second plate with 8 legs and 1 whole head shell, and a third plate containing the remaining legs, the parts joining all the legs to the head, the fragments of claw shell and the remaining head.
5 Crush the contents of the third plate roughly with a meat bat or the back of a very large, heavy knife.
6 Melt the butter in a saucepan, add the finely diced onions and sliced chillies and sauté gently for 2–3 minutes without browning. Add the lemon rind, turmeric and dried basil, mix carefully, then add the crushed carcases on plate three.
7 Stir again and heat through for 3–4 minutes before adding the water. Continue to cook on a low heat, stirring continuously until all the water has evaporated. Add the coconut milk, season lightly with salt and reduce over a moderate heat for 5 minutes.
8 Strain the sauce through a fine wire sieve into another saucepan, pressing the lobster shells carefully with the back of a large spoon or ladle to extract all the juices and coconut milk.
9 Bring this to a gentle simmer, add the diced courgettes, bring to the boil and simmer gently for 5 minutes. Taste and add a little salt and pepper if necessary.
10 Put the remaining head on a board with the underside facing upwards, and with a large, heavy knife, cut through the shell down the centre, from top to bottom. Lay the two halves, insides facing upwards, on a tray. If you look carefully at the top section of the head, just behind

the eyes, you will find a sack (it should be cut in half). Remove and discard this sack. Now place the legs on the tray also and put into a hot oven or under a warm grill for a few minutes to heat through.

11 Just before serving, put the lobster flesh into the sauce, add the lemon juice and cook for a minute or two. Divide the sauce between two plates and garnish each plate with 4 legs each and half the reserved head.

Note: It is important that the lobster flesh is not overcooked, as this will most certainly make it rather tough. You may substitute a ¼ teaspoon chilli powder for the fresh chillies, but the flavours will change and, anyway, if you have taken all the trouble to buy and prepare the lobster, a little extra effort to obtain fresh chillies won't hurt.

CRAB NEST

For 4–6 people
Preparation time 35 minutes
Cooking time 25 minutes

To pick the meat out of a crab is a real labour of love but well worth the effort. The flavour and texture are almost equal to that of lobster and certainly much cheaper. The large crabs with angry claws found all around the British coast are delicious, especially if you choose a female with her berry – a brilliant coral-red roe that looks and tastes wonderful.

150 g/5 oz crab meat, cooked
110g/4 oz rice vermicelli (see note)
vegetable oil for deep-frying
1 clove garlic, crushed
110 g/4 oz French beans, cut into 1-cm/½-inch pieces
50 g/2 oz carrots, finely diced
75 g/3 oz button mushrooms, sliced
225 ml/8 fl oz water
225 ml/8 fl oz double cream
10 g/½ oz cornflour
½ teaspoon sugar
salt and freshly ground pepper
2 eggs, lightly beaten

1 Deep-fry the vermicelli in hot oil until crisp. Drain on kitchen paper towel and arrange into a nest on a large plate.

2 Put 2 tablespoons of the hot oil into a saucepan and fry the garlic over a gentle heat until it starts to brown slightly.

3 Add the French beans and cook for 2–3 minutes, then add the carrots. Continue to cook for a further 2 minutes before adding the mushrooms, then cook, stirring, for a minute or two.

4 Remove the vegetables from the pan and keep warm.

5 Mix the water, cream, cornflour and sugar together, adding a little salt and pepper to taste.

6 Pour into a hot pan, quickly whisk in the beaten eggs and continue whisking gently until the sauce is thick. This will only take a minute.

7 Add the crab meat, blend in to mix and heat through.

8 Spoon this mixture over the vermicelli nest and garnish with the cooked vegetables. Serve immediately.

Note: Known as *laksa* in Malaysia, rice vermicelli – also called rice sticks or rice noodles – are used in many different ways and come in various shapes and sizes, from the thin string-like variety called *bun* for the above recipe, to the thicker egg noodles. The different sizes can be interchanged in recipes if the specified type is difficult to obtain.

WHITE CURRY

For 4–6 people
Preparation time 30 minutes
Cooking time 35 minutes

This is a deliciously mild, rich curry with a base of coconut milk, much loved by Indonesians. I would recommend this dish for those taking their first tentative steps into Asian cuisine.

1 kg/2 lb large Mediterranean prawns, cooked
1 tablespoon butter
225 g/8 oz onions, finely diced
2 cloves garlic, crushed
1 teaspoon finely grated fresh ginger
¼ teaspoon chilli powder
1 teaspoon ground turmeric
4 bay leaves
425 ml/¾ pint coconut milk *(see page 105)*
1 teaspoon salt
lemon juice to taste

1 Shell and devein the prawns if preferred, but I believe that the prawns should remain in their shells for this recipe.
2 Heat the butter in a saucepan and gently fry the onions for 3 minutes. Add the garlic and ginger and continue to cook for a minute longer.
3 Add the chilli powder, turmeric and bay leaves and fry for a further minute.
4 Pour in the coconut milk and salt and bring to simmering point, stirring continuously. Reduce the heat and allow to simmer gently, uncovered, for 20 minutes.
5 Add the prawns and allow to cook for 10 minutes without increasing the heat.
6 Remove from the heat, add lemon juice to taste and serve immediately.

Note: Do not at any time cover the pan during cooking. The liquid should be stirred continuously while coming to the boil to prevent curdling.

Two fresh chillies, deseeded and sliced, give a better flavour than the chilli powder.

CURRIED PRAWNS WITH CUCUMBER

For 4–6 people
Preparation time 30 minutes
Cooking time 15 minutes

This dish came to me from the Indonesian quarter of Amsterdam. The gentleman who gave it to me swore that he was a descendant of one of the great ruling families of Indonesia and that his cooks had created this dish. He also said that he would sell it to me for a small sum . . . The recipe was a disaster but the idea for the unusual combination of ingredients intrigued me, so I went ahead and developed my own version.

1 Put the anchovy, garlic, spring onions and oil into a blender and purée until smooth.
2 Heat a deep pan until hot, then add the purée and all the spices and sauté gently for 3 minutes.
3 Stir in the coconut milk and bring to the boil. Turn down the heat to low and simmer for 5 minutes.
4 Add the cucumber, lemon rind and juice and sugar and cook until the cucumber is translucent, approximately 5 minutes.
5 Put in the prawns, bring to the boil and serve immediately.

450 g/1 lb peeled prawns, cooked
2 anchovy fillets
1 clove garlic
3 spring onions, chopped
55 ml/2 fl oz vegetable oil
½ teaspoon ground ginger
1 teaspoon ground fennel
2 teaspoons ground coriander
1 teaspoon turmeric
1 teaspoon chilli powder
425 ml/¾ pint coconut milk (see page 105)
1 medium cucumber, peeled, quartered lengthways and seeds removed, then cut into thick sticks
2 teaspoons grated lemon rind
juice of 1 lemon
1 teaspoon sugar

SPICED MUSSELS

For 4 people
Preparation time 45 minutes
Cooking time 30 minutes

One of the joys of provincial French cuisine is moules marinières. *I adapted this recipe using the same technique but in what I hope is the Asian way.*

1 Scrub the mussels well, making sure you beard them also.
2 Heat the butter in a large pan and sauté the onions for 5 minutes. Add the garlic and ginger and fry for a minute or two more.
3 Add the turmeric, coriander and chilli powder and continue to fry, stirring, for 2 minutes.
4 Pour in the water, add the salt and bring to the boil. Cover and simmer for 5 minutes.
5 Throw in the mussels, cover and cook for 10–15 minutes, or until the shells have opened.
6 Remove from the heat, sprinkle in the parsley and lemon juice. Stir well.
7 Transfer the mussels to deep plates and pour the sauce over them and serve.

Note: If the fresh mussels are not tightly closed when raw, tap them sharply on a hard surface. If they close, they are fine, if not, they are dead and should be discarded. Discard any mussels that are not open after being cooked for the prescribed time.

Add 2 fresh red chillies, deseeded and finely sliced, to this recipe at step 3 to give extra flavour.

1 kg/2 lb fresh mussels
50 g/2 oz unsalted butter
225 g/8 oz onions, diced
3 cloves garlic
½ teaspoon ground ginger
½ teaspoon ground turmeric
2 teaspoons ground coriander
a pinch of chilli powder
275 ml/½ pint water
½ teaspoon salt
1 tablespoon chopped parsley
juice of ½ lemon

INDONESIAN SQUID

For 4 people
Preparation time 1 hour
Cooking time 25 minutes

The squid is a strange creature, lacking in allure, and on first impressions the leathery exterior seems unappetizing. In reality, however, it ranks as the most delicious of foods and in Southeast Asia and the Far East plays an important role in cookery. Squid is delicious to eat as long as you follow the principle that the cooking must be either very brief or very long – anything between, and your squid will be as tough as leather. As a general rule, the smaller the squid, the more tender and sweet it is. The larger ones can be improved by marinating in wine vinegar with sliced onion, salt and pepper for several hours.

12 small squid
2 teaspoons ground almonds
½ teaspoon chilli powder
2 cloves garlic, crushed
110 g/4 oz onions, diced
2 anchovy fillets
30 ml/1 fl oz vegetable oil
½ teaspoon grated lime or lemon rind
55 ml/2 fl oz lime or lemon juice
55 ml/2 fl oz white wine vinegar
25 g/1 oz soft brown sugar
2 teaspoons paprika
salt

1 First prepare the squid. Hold the squid in one hand and with the other reach inside the body and pull the head and tentacles away.
2 Pull off the mottled skin that covers the body to expose the white, almost transparent flesh. Discard the skin.
3 Feel inside the body for the transparent cartilage, draw it out and discard.
4 Wash the body thoroughly inside and out under cold running water and separate the two flaps at the tail end, which pull away easily as they are only held in place by suction.
5 Cut the tentacles away from the head. The head, which contains the entrails, can now be discarded.
6 Cut the body into rings, slice the flaps and chop the tentacles to a manageable size. The squid is now ready to cook.
7 Put the almonds, chilli powder, garlic, onions, anchovy fillets and oil into a blender and blend to a smooth paste.
8 Heat a large, deep frying pan and, when hot, add the almond mixture and lime or lemon rind and sauté gently for 2 minutes.
9 Add the lime or lemon juice, wine vinegar, sugar and paprika and continue to cook for a further 10 minutes, stirring constantly.
10 Add the squid and cook for 10 minutes, stirring occasionally.
11 Season to taste with salt, transfer to a warm serving dish and serve at once.

Meat Dishes

In an area of such size and cultural diversity, there are bound to be many distinctive dishes belonging to different regions. Some say the most impressive and tastiest dishes belong to Sumatra and Java – although cooks in other regions may disagree. Nonetheless, cooks in Sumatra are renowned for their creativity and they use every known dried spice, combined with onions, chillies, garlic, fresh herbs, coconut milk, tarmarind and ground white nuts to make their fragrant curry sauces, which contain the meat, lung, brains and liver of the buffalo, poultry, seafood, vegetables and fruit.

Fresh green chillies are served as side dishes, or blended together with other ingredients to make varying sambals, *which are served with every meal in Indonesia. Most dishes are mildly seasoned, but the hot* sambal *adds as much extra 'pain' as one needs.*

Eating with utensils in the Western tradition is practical, as most food is cut into bite-sized chunks before being cooked. Duck and chicken is generally served on the bone, but for the benefit of those who prefer not to use their fingers I have introduced recipes that do not call for the grappling and gnawing of bones. Another interesting factor is that Asians do not mind eating food that is meant to be hot cold; indeed, many times has the food that was served early in the evening been enjoyed in the small hours by myself and friends, without any of it being reheated.

CHICKEN CROQUETTES WITH SPICY SAUCE

For 4–6 people
Preparation time 30 minutes
Cooking time 15 minutes

700 g/1½ lb chicken, including skin and fat
25 g/1 oz unsalted butter
175 g/6 oz onions, finely diced
110 g/4 oz white breadcrumbs, moistened with a little milk
1 teaspoon ground ginger
1 egg yolk
2 tablespoons chopped parsley
salt and freshly ground pepper
oil for deep-frying
cornflour for coating

This is a marvellous way of using up leftover pieces of fresh chicken meat.

1 Remove the bones from the chicken and pass the flesh through a fine mincer or food processor.
2 Melt the butter in a pan and fry the onions gently until soft.
3 Add the cooked onions to the minced chicken, together with the breadcrumbs, ginger, egg yolk and parsley and season with salt and pepper. Mix well.
4 Heat the oil in a deep pan until very hot.
5 With wet hands, shape the chicken mixture into cylindrical shapes, dust lightly with cornflour and deep-fry until golden brown. Drain on kitchen paper towel and serve with the following sauce.
Note: To vary the shape of the croquettes, try forming pear or apple shapes and sticking a piece of uncooked spaghetti into the top for the stalk and then deep-frying.

SPICY SAUCE

110 g/4 oz pineapple and apple chutney *(see page 113)*
55 ml/2 fl oz soy sauce
55 ml/2 fl oz water
1 teaspoon grated ginger

1 Purée the chutney in a food processor.
2 Transfer to a pan and add the soy sauce, water and ginger.
3 Bring to the boil and simmer for 5 minutes.
4 Serve warm with the hot chicken croquettes.
Note: Worcestershire sauce can be used in place of soy sauce, but add a little tomato ketchup.

GRILLED CHICKEN IN COCONUT SAUCE

For 2 people
Preparation time 30 minutes
Cooking time 25 minutes

450 g/1 lb chicken breasts
50 g/2 oz onions, diced
2 cloves garlic
25 g/1 oz ground almonds
1 teaspoon ground coriander
½ teaspoon chilli powder
½ teaspoon turmeric
1 tablespoon vegetable oil
570 ml/1 pint coconut milk (see page 105)
1 bay leaf
grated rind of 1 lemon
salt

1 Crush the onions and garlic in a mortar or heavy bowl, then mix in the ground almonds to make a paste.
2 Add the coriander, chilli powder and turmeric and stir thoroughly until all the ingredients are well blended into a thick paste.
3 Heat the oil in a large saucepan and sauté the paste for 20 seconds over a high heat. Put in the chicken breasts and brown on both sides, making sure they are well coated with the oil and paste. Remove the breasts from the pan and set aside.
4 Pour the coconut milk into the pan, add the bay leaf and grated lemon rind. Bring to the boil, then simmer gently, uncovered, until the sauce thickens almost to the consistency of double cream. Season to taste with salt.
5 To serve, heat the grill to high and cook the chicken breasts 7–10 minutes on one side and 5 minutes on the other. When cooked, remove to warm plates and spoon over a little sauce. Serve immediately.
Note: For the truly adventurous, and those with insulated mouths, instead of using chilli powder, add 6 fresh green chillies just after the coconut cream starts to boil. Serve this dish with plain boiled rice, blanched carrots and beans.

GRILLED SPICED CHICKEN

For 4 people
Preparation time 20 minutes
Cooking time 45 minutes

4 chicken legs, skin removed
½ teaspoon chilli powder
2 teaspoons turmeric
1 tablespoon coriander seeds
40 g/1½ oz blanched almonds
3 cloves garlic
1 teaspoon grated lemon rind
½ teaspoon salt
1 teaspoon sugar
2–3 tablespoons water
55 ml/2 fl oz vegetable oil
275 ml/½ pint coconut milk (see page 105)
juice of 1 lemon

1 Put all the spices, almonds, garlic, lemon rind, salt and sugar into a blender, adding a tablespoon of water, and blend to a smooth paste – add a little more water if required.
2 Heat the oil in a large frying pan and sauté the spice paste over a medium heat for 5 minutes, stirring constantly.
3 Stir in the coconut milk and chicken legs and bring to the boil. Cover, reduce the heat to low and cook for 20 minutes.
4 Remove the cover, add the lemon juice and continue cooking for a further 10 minutes. At this stage, the liquid should almost be evaporated and thick; if not, continue cooking a little longer.
5 Preheat the grill to high. Place the chicken pieces on a rack in the grill pan and grill for 5 minutes each side, or until they are nice and brown, basting with the remainder of the cooking liquid. Serve at once.
Note: Read my comments on the use of coriander seeds (see page 124). The addition of 2 green chillies at step 1 and, if available, ½ teaspoon of Laos or Galingale powder will make this dish more original. The dish can be prepared the day before up to step 5. Leave it to cool in the sauce, then grill before serving.

BALINESE CHICKEN

For 4 people
Preparation time 20 minutes
Cooking time 40 minutes

4 chicken breasts, skin and bones removed
salt and pepper
flour for dusting
55 ml/2 fl oz peanut or vegetable oil
110 g/4 oz onions, diced
2 cloves garlic, crushed
4 brazil nuts chopped, or 12 almonds
½ teaspoon chilli powder
½ teaspoon ground ginger
275 ml/½ pint coconut milk (see page 105)
1 tablespoon soy sauce
1 teaspoon soft brown sugar
1 teaspoon wine vinegar

1 Season the chicken breasts with salt and pepper on both sides. Dust in flour and set aside.
2 Heat the oil in a large, deep frying pan and quickly fry the chicken breasts lightly on both sides, remove and keep warm.
3 Purée the onions, garlic, nuts, chilli powder and ginger in a blender with a little of the coconut milk until it is a smooth paste. Place the paste in a frying pan and sauté over a high heat for 5 minutes, stirring continuously.
4 Add the remaining coconut milk, soy sauce, sugar and vinegar and quickly bring to the boil. Reduce the heat to low and simmer gently.
5 Transfer the chicken breasts to the pan and simmer for 20 minutes, uncovered, basting the breasts thoroughly with the liquid. Season to taste with salt and pepper and serve immediately.

CHICKEN AND MANGO CASSEROLE

For 4 people
Preparation time 20 minutes
Cooking time 50 minutes

Anton Mosimann, the Maître Chef at the Dorchester Hotel, Park Lane, London, gave me the idea for this dish during my time spent in his kitchen in 1982. It combines two of the favourite Southeast Asian foods – chicken and mango – and this smooth, rich and spicy dish would be equally well received in Park Lane or some isolated kampong *in Indonesia.*

4 chicken breasts, skin and bones removed
1 mango, peeled and sliced (discard the stone)
salt and pepper
flour for dusting
55 ml/2 fl oz peanut or vegetable oil
225 g/8 oz onions, finely diced
grated rind of 1 lemon
¼ teaspoon ground coriander
¼ teaspoon ground cinnamon
275 ml/½ pint chicken stock (see page 9)
150 ml/¼ pint double cream
1 tablespoon lemon juice

1 Preheat the oven to 190°C/375°F/Gas Mark 5.
2 Season the chicken breasts with salt and pepper on both sides and dust with flour.
3 Heat the oil in a frying pan and, when hot, fry the chicken breasts on both sides until lightly browned. Remove the breasts to a casserole dish and set aside.
4 Add the onions to the frying pan and gently sauté for 5 minutes, stirring occasionally, or until soft. Remove with a slotted spoon and place the onions on top of the chicken breasts.
5 Sauté the mango slices in the same pan for 2 minutes on both sides, stirring in the lemon rind, coriander and cinnamon, then add the chicken stock and bring to the boil, stirring constantly.
6 Pour this over the chicken breasts in the casserole, cover and place in the oven and cook for 20 minutes.
7 Remove from the pan and carefully drain off all the liquid into a deep frying pan. Turn the oven off and return the casserole with the chicken breasts to the oven to keep hot.
8 Bring the contents of the pan to the boil and continue fast boiling to evaporate and reduce the liquid by half.
9 Add the cream and continue boiling until the sauce starts to thicken, then turn down the heat to low and simmer gently.
9 Transfer the contents of the casserole to a warm serving plate. Add the lemon juice to the thick cream sauce, season to taste, stir well and pour the sauce over the chicken breasts and mango. Serve at once.
Note: Read my comments on the use of coriander (see page 124).

INDONESIAN CHICKEN

For 6 people
Preparation time 20 minutes
Marinating time 30 minutes
Cooking time approximately 1 hour

This is a typical Indonesian dish consisting of small chicken portions set in a rich sauce, which would be placed in the centre of the table with all the other accompaniments and diners would help themselves, using their fingers. A delightful way of eating!

2 kg/4 lb chicken
55 ml/2 fl oz wine vinegar, red or white
25 g/1 oz soft brown sugar
1 teaspoon salt
55 ml/2 fl oz peanut or vegetable oil

For the sauce
225 g/8 oz onions, peeled and finely diced
a pinch of chilli powder or cayenne pepper
2 cloves garlic, crushed
225 ml/8 fl oz water
1 tablespoon wine vinegar, white or red
30 ml/1 fl oz soy sauce
1 tablespoon sugar, white
6 tomatoes, peeled, deseeded and chopped

1 Remove all the skin from the chicken, then cut into 12 equal portions (2 wings, each breast cut into three, each thigh in half and 2 drumsticks).
2 Put the wine vinegar, soft brown sugar and salt into a bowl and whisk well to blend the ingredients. Put in the chicken pieces, coat well and set aside for 30 minutes.
3 Put all the ingredients for the sauce, except the tomatoes, into a blender and blend until smooth. Transfer to a large saucepan, bring to the boil, turn down the heat to low, cover and simmer gently for 10 minutes.
4 Heat the oil in a frying pan and, when hot, brown the chicken pieces all over, then transfer the pieces to kitchen paper towel to drain.
5 Place the chicken pieces in the simmering sauce, add the diced tomatoes and mix well. Cover and simmer for 25–30 minutes.
6 Remove the cover from the saucepan and allow to simmer for a further 10–15 minutes or until about a third of the liquid has evaporated.
7 Arrange on a warm serving plate and serve immediately.
Note: A whole green chilli may be substituted for the chilli powder or cayenne pepper, but this will, of course, make it much hotter.

PENANG CHICKEN

For 8 people
Preparation time 15 minutes
Cooking time 50 minutes

Penang is a green fortress of an island off the west coast of Malaysia. I fell in love with this island at first sight and, although I have never had the chance to return, its magic still lingers. This recipe came from an old resident my uncle introduced to me and I have carried it with me ever since.

1 Fry the onions and garlic gently in the oil in a deep frying pan for 5 minutes, stirring occasionally, then sprinkle on the turmeric.
2 Add the sugar and continue cooking until the sugar starts to caramelize and the onions go brown.
3 Stir in the chicken pieces and fry for 10 minutes, turning frequently, or until they become a deep brown.
4 Add the remaining ingredients, adding salt to taste, then bring to the boil. Cover, reduce the heat to low and simmer for 10 minutes.
5 Remove the cover, increase the heat slightly and cook the chicken for a further 20 minutes, or until you feel it is cooked through. Serve immediately.
Note: Half a green or red pepper, diced, may be used instead of chilli powder to reduce the fire in this dish. Alternatively, 2 red or green chillies, finely chopped, may be added to turn it into the authentic Penang chicken.

2 chickens (approximately 1.5 kg/3lb each) cut into 8 portions
450 g/1 lb onions, finely diced
2 cloves garlic, crushed
55 ml/2 fl oz vegetable oil
1 teaspoon turmeric
1 tablespoon soft brown sugar
½ teaspoon chilli powder
55 ml/2 fl oz soy sauce
55 ml/2 fl oz wine vinegar, white or red
30 ml/1 fl oz water
salt

CAPTAIN'S CURRY

For 4 people
Preparation time 20 minutes
Cooking time approximately 45 minutes

How this curry got its name is lost somewhere in mythology. There are countless variations of this dish throughout Southeast Asia, ranging from a recipe full of fiery green chillies to the subtle flavours of coconut and spices. This is my gentler version.

1 Remove all the skin from the chicken and set aside. Carefully remove all the flesh from the bones of the chicken and cut into approximately 2.5-cm/1-inch cubes. (You can make a good stock or soup with the skin and bones.)
2 Heat the oil in a saucepan and, when hot, gently fry the onions and garlic until soft. Add all the ground spices and ground almonds and continue frying for 3 minutes longer. If the spice mixture starts to dry out too much, add a tablespoon of water.
3 Add the chicken pieces and turn over in the spice mixture. Pour on the coconut milk, sprinkle in the sugar, add a pinch of salt and pepper to taste, then cover and simmer gently for 20 minutes or until the chicken pieces are tender.
4 Transfer the chicken pieces to a serving dish and keep warm. bring the sauce back to the boil, reduce the heat and simmer gently for 10 more minutes or until the sauce thickens slightly.
5 Pour on top of the chicken pieces and serve garnished with the spring onions.
Note: The hotter version of Captain's Curry is to add 2 finely chopped green chillies at step 2, and 4 whole green chillies at step 3.

1.5 kg/3 lb chicken
2 tablespoons vegetable oil.
110 g/4 oz onions, finely diced
3 cloves garlic, crushed
½ teaspoon ground ginger
1 tablespoon ground coriander
1 teaspoon ground cumin
1 teaspoon turmeric
¼ teaspoon ground nutmeg
¼ teaspoon ground cinnamon
¼ teaspoon ground cardamom
1 tablespoon ground almonds
350 ml/12 fl oz coconut milk (see page 105)
1 teaspoon sugar
salt and freshly ground pepper
4 spring onions, chopped (optional)

CHICKEN LIVER SATAY

For 4 people
Preparation time 20 minutes
Marinating time 1 hour
Cooking time 35 minutes

450 g/1 lb chicken livers
110 g/4 oz onions, finely diced
4 cloves garlic, crushed
½ teaspoon ground ginger
110 ml/4 fl oz natural yoghurt
1 teaspoon salt
2 teaspoons vegetable oil

Sauce
350 g/12 oz onions, finely diced
50 g/2 oz butter
6 cloves garlic, crushed
½ teaspoon ground ginger
1 tablespoon ground coriander
1 teaspoon ground cumin
1 teaspoon turmeric
¼ teaspoon chilli powder
2 large tomatoes, skinned and chopped
55 ml/2 fl oz water
½ tablespoon chopped parsley
1 teaspoon garam masala

1 Mix together the onions, garlic, ginger, yoghurt, salt and vegetable oil in a deep bowl.
2 Clean the chicken livers by cutting away the sinews and any green blemishes (galls). Add to the marinade and set aside for 1 hour.
3 Prepare the sauce by frying the onions in butter for 10 minutes without browning, then add the garlic and fry for 5 minutes more over a low heat.
4 Add the ginger, coriander, cumin, turmeric, chilli, tomatoes and water. Bring to the boil, turn down the heat and simmer, covered, for 10 minutes.
5 Remove the chicken livers from the marinade and thread onto skewers.
6 Add the marinade to the sauce, stirring it well in. Bring to the boil and simmer, uncovered, for about 5 minutes, adding the parsley and garam masala halfway through.
7 Grill the chicken livers, turning regularly for 10 minutes.
8 Serve on a bed of boiled rice with the sauce and a simple green salad.
Note: I particularly like this dish with the *satay* on top of a *chapati* and some sauce spooned over.

RAJAH'S CHICKEN SATAY

For 4–6 people
Preparation time 20 minutes
Marinating time overnight
Cooking time 20–30 minutes

In some parts of the world, I am still affectionately known as Rajah – not a hereditary title, just a nickname given to me by a remarkable Scotsman. This dish is somewhat similar to the tandoori chicken of north India, but I have adapted it for the barbecue and grill instead of the traditional tandoori ovens. This is the satay *I generally entertain my friends with, because of its exquisite taste and colour.*

1 Put the yoghurt and all the other ingredients in a deep bowl and mix well. Add the chicken meat and stir to coat all the pieces. Cover with plastic cling film and refrigerate overnight.
2 Heat the grill to medium high, thread the meat onto skewers and cook gently for 20–30 minutes, basting and turning frequently.
3 Serve with a salad of sliced tomatoes and cucumber with chopped onion and mint leaves. Sprinkle this with salt, black pepper and a little olive oil and lemon juice.

1 kg/2 lb chicken breasts and thighs, skin and bones removed and cubed
225 ml/8 fl oz natural yoghurt
6 cloves garlic, crushed
1 teaspoon ground ginger
1 teaspoon ground cumin
½ teaspoon ground nutmeg
1 teaspoon garam masala
¼ teaspoon ground cloves
¼ teaspoon chilli powder
2 tablespoons vegetable oil
2 teaspoon salt
¼ teaspoon red food colouring

CHICKEN SATAY

For 4–6 people
Preparation time 15 minutes
Marinating time 2 hours
Cooking time 20 minutes

1 Combine the ingredients for the marinade in a suitable bowl, put the chicken cubes into it and set aside for 2 hours.
2 Place all the ingredients for the sauce except the water in a liquidizer and purée until smooth.
3 Bring the water to the boil and add the mixture from the liquidizer, stirring well. Simmer until the sauce is thick, about 5–10 minutes. Check for seasoning and add more salt if necessary.
4 While the sauce is simmering, put the chicken cubes onto thin bamboo (if you have them) or metal skewers and grill them for 10 minutes under a hot grill, turning occasionally.
5 Serve hot with the sauce on the side.
Note: Traditionally, *Longtong* (compressed boiled rice), always eaten cold, is served with this dish.

1 kg/2 lb chicken breasts, cut into 2-cm/¾-inch cubes

For the marinade
3 tablespoons soy sauce
3 tablespoons vegetable oil
1 teaspoon caster sugar

For the sauce
110 g/4 oz peanuts (roasted)
3 tablespoons soy sauce
2 cloves garlic
1 tablespoon diced onion
1 tablespoon lemon juice
1 teaspoon brown sugar
salt to taste
175 ml/6 fl oz water

LAMB SATAY

For 4–6 people
Preparation time 30 minutes
Marinating time overnight
Cooking time 20 minutes

1 kg/2 lb lamb (boned leg of lamb is best), cut into 2.5-cm/1-inch cubes
110 g/4 oz onions, finely chopped or minced
1 clove garlic
½ teaspoon ground ginger
2 tablespoons soy sauce
2 teaspoons ground coriander
2 tablespoons red wine vinegar
1 tablespoon vegetable oil

Sauce
110 g/4 oz roasted, unsalted peanuts
1 tablespoon cooking oil
110 g/4 oz onions, diced
1 clove garlic, crushed
½ teaspoon chilli powder
4 anchovy fillets, finely chopped
275 ml/½ pint water
1 teaspoon brown sugar
1 teaspoon salt
1 tablespoon lemon juice

1 Put the chopped or minced onions into a deep bowl with the garlic, ginger, soy sauce, coriander, wine vinegar and oil. Add the pieces of lamb and mix well. Cover with plastic cling film and refrigerate overnight.
2 To make the sauce, grind the peanuts to a powder in a pestle and mortar or food processor.
3 Heat the oil in a frying pan and sauté the onions gently for 5 minutes. Add the garlic, chilli powder and the anchovy fillets. Cook gently for 3 minutes without browning.
4 Add the water, ground peanuts, sugar, salt and lemon juice. Bring to the boil, turn down the heat and simmer gently until the sauce thickens, about 10 minutes. Set aside.
5 Thread the meat onto skewers and grill for 5–10 minutes, turning frequently.
6 Serve on a bed of plain boiled rice, with a little of the reheated sauce spooned on top.
Note: I always insist on lamb being served pink. The grilling time for the above *satay* is suited to my taste, but that doesn't mean that it cannot be cooked any longer. All *satays* are ideal for barbecues, but this one needs a gentle heat, somewhere on the edges of the charcoal.

LAMB GULE

For 4 people
Preparation time 20 minutes
Cooking time 50 minutes

Lamb Gule is a very liquid dish, almost like meaty soup. I can remember my mother serving us with a great bowl of rice filled to the brim with Gule, and we would all sit on the floor around this bowl and tuck in with large tablespoons. Marvellous!

Rajah's Chicken Satay (see page 48) *and Lamb Satay*

450 g/1 lb lamb, cut into cubes
110 g/4 oz onions, diced
2 cloves garlic
1 teaspoon ground coriander
1 teaspoon turmeric
½ teaspoon chilli powder
½ teaspoon ground allspice
½ teaspoon ground ginger
grated rind of 1 lemon
grated rind of 1 orange
2 tablespoons vegetable oil
275 ml/½ pint water
1 tablespoon wine vinegar
1 tablespoon brown sugar
2 bay leaves
570 ml/1 pint thick coconut milk (see page 105)
salt

1 Crush the onions and garlic in a mortar. Add the coriander, turmeric, chilli powder, allspice, ginger, lemon and orange rind and mix together well to form a paste.
2 Heat the oil in a deep pan and fry the paste over a high heat for 1 minute. Add the meat and fry for 2 minutes, stirring to coat the pieces with the spices.
3 Add all the other ingredients *except* the coconut milk and salt.
4 Bring to the boil. Cover and simmer until the lamb is tender, 30–45 minutes.
5 Add the thick coconut milk stirring continuously until the first bubbles appear at boiling point. Remove from the heat immediately.
6 Taste and add salt if necesssary. Remove the bay leaves and serve.
Note: Thick coconut milk will curdle at boiling point and spoil the dish. If you feel that the stew is too watery for your taste, do not thicken with flour, but reduce the amount of water or use thicker coconut milk.

This dish can be prepared in advance up to step 4 and kept in the refrigerator without spoiling for 5–6 days, as long as the coconut milk has not been added. To serve, just reheat and add the coconut milk.

LAMB STEAKS WITH YOGHURT, CUCUMBER AND MINT

For 4 people
Preparation time 15 minutes
Cooking time 20 minutes

4 lamb steaks
1 tablespoon olive oil
salt and freshly ground black pepper
1 small cucumber
150 ml/¼ pint natural yoghurt
1 small onion, finely diced
3 teaspoons finely chopped fresh mint
2 bunches mint leaves to garnish

1 Brush the lamb steaks with olive oil and season both sides with salt and pepper and set aside.
2 Preheat the grill until very hot. Place the steaks under the grill and cook for 2 minutes each side.
3 Lower the heat by half and continue cooking for a further 5–7 minutes on each side, basting frequently.
4 Peel the cucumber and scoop out the seeds with a teaspoon. Discard the seeds. Dice the flesh and set aside.
5 Pour the yoghurt into a bowl and beat lightly with a whisk until smooth and creamy.
6 Add the diced onion, diced cucumber and chopped mint. Season to taste. Stir thoroughly to mix well.
7 Arrange the mint leaves on warm plates, place the lamb steaks on top and serve immediately with the sauce served separately in individual sauce boats.
Note: This sauce can be made well in advance and stored in the refrigerator. It can be used for all sorts of spiced dishes. To 'liven up' the flavour, at step 7 add a pinch of cayenne pepper and ¼ teaspoon ground, roasted cumin seeds.

SPICED ROAST LAMB

For 6–8 people
Preparation time 30–40 minutes
Marinating time 4 hours or overnight
Cooking time 2½ hours

This dish has its origins in the Mogul Empire and its lavish taste reflects the richness of Persian culinary traditions. Obviously it has been adapted to suit 'local' tastes and I have attempted to keep to the Asian recipe.

2.25 kg/5 lb leg of lamb, bone removed
4 teaspoons cumin seeds
20 black peppercorns
10 cloves
1 stick cinnamon (approximately 10 cm/4 inches long)
3 whole bay leaves, dried
10 cardamom pods
570 ml/1 pint natural yoghurt
1 teaspoon ground ginger
8 cloves garlic, crushed
a pinch of chilli powder
2 tablespoons chopped parsley
2 teaspoons salt
175 g/6 oz butter

1 Trim all the fat off the lamb. Make sure the skin has been pulled off.
2 Grind the cumin seeds, black peppercorns, cloves, cinnamon, bay leaves and cardamom in a pestle and mortar or an electric grinder.
3 Pour the yoghurt into a large bowl and add the ground spices, mixing them in together well with the ginger, garlic, chilli powder, parsley and salt.
4 Place the lamb in the bowl with the marinade, making sure you coat it well. Set it aside for a minimum of 4 hours, but preferably overnight, turning occasionally.
5 Melt the butter in a roasting pan and brush over the lamb. Place the meat in the pan and pour on the marinade. Cover with foil.
6 Bake at 180°C/350°F/Gas Mark 4 for about 2½ hours, basting frequently.
7 Add more salt if required. Cut into slices and serve.
Note: For once I have stipulated the use of fresh dried spices. For a better flavour, these spices can be gently heated before being ground, to bring out their full flavour and heavenly aromas so that they penetrate deep into the lamb and sauce. Preground spices may be used, and will impart nearly the same flavour, but will lack that little extra something that makes this dish outstanding.

Try using this recipe for a Sunday lunch and serving it with boiled or baked potatoes and plenty of salad. It is also delicious eaten cold.

MINTED LEG OF LAMB

For 6–8 people
Preparation time 30 minutes
Cooking time 2 hours

Mint appears in countless preparations from China to the Mediterranean. In England, mint is traditionally used with roast lamb in the form of a jelly or sauce. Here we have mint used in a marinade to bring out all the unusual flavours of the East.

2.25 kg/5 lb leg of lamb
75 g/3 oz mint leaves
½ teaspoon ground ginger
3 cloves garlic, crushed
350 g/12 oz onions, diced
50 g/2 oz green pepper (capsicum), diced
1½ teaspoons salt
150 ml/¼ pint honey
juice of 1 lemon
110 g/4 oz butter, melted

1 Remove as much fat as possible from the leg of lamb and make sure the skin has been pulled off. Cut deep incisions into the meat, right down to the bone, at regular intervals. Place in a deep baking tray.
2 Put all the other ingredients into a blender and liquidize.
3 Cover the meat with the purée, making sure you work the liquid into the incisions.
4 Cover with foil and bake in a preheated 200°C/400°F/Gas Mark 6 oven for 30 minutes, then reduce to 180°C/350°F/Gas Mark 4 for a further 1½ hours or until the lamb is cooked, basting at regular intervals.
5 Carve into slices and serve with rice and salad.

SAVOURY LAMB PANCAKES

For 8–10 people
Preparation time 20 minutes
Resting time 1 hour
Cooking time 1 hour

350 g/12 oz wholewheat flour
a good pinch of salt
225 ml/8 fl oz hot water
55 ml/2 fl oz vegetable oil
1 egg, beaten

For the filling
55 ml/2 fl oz vegetable oil
225 g/8 oz onions, finely diced
1 clove garlic, crushed
350 g/12 oz minced lamb
½ teaspoon chilli powder
1 large tomato, peeled and diced
50 g/2 oz sweetcorn (canned or frozen)
salt and freshly ground pepper
1 teaspoon garam masala

1 To make the dough, sift the flour and salt into a deep bowl and make a well in the centre. Pour in the water and beat quickly until a stiff dough is formed. Cover and set aside to rest for 1 hour.
2 To make the filling, heat the oil in a frying pan and sauté the onions gently for 5 minutes. Add the garlic and cook for 1 minute longer, stirring to prevent browning.
3 Stir in the lamb and chilli powder and cook for a further 3 minutes.
4 Add the tomato and sweetcorn, stir well and cook for a further 3 minutes. Reduce the heat to low and simmer for 10 minutes.
5 Season to taste with salt and pepper, sprinkle over the garam masala and stir well. Remove from the heat and keep warm.
6 Remove the dough from the bowl and knead gently for 20 seconds.
7 Slightly oil the work surface and divide the dough into 8 or 10 equal balls, pressing each ball out with the heel of the hand into a very thin, almost strudel-like pancake.
8 Heat a little of the oil in a frying pan, brushing to coat the whole surface. When hot, put in a pancake and brush over the exposed surface with a little beaten egg, spoon over some filling then fold over the side of the pancake to form a 'D' shape. Seal the edges so that the filling is completely enclosed and fry for 1 minute. Remove from the pan and proceed as above until all the pancakes are made.
9 Heat in a hot oven for 10 minutes, then serve as a starter or a snack.
Note: Leftover lamb, minced, is also good to use in this recipe, but omit the 10 minutes cooking time at step 4. Green peas or diced French beans can be substituted for sweetcorn, and 2 green chillies finely sliced, may be used instead of chilli powder. If you don't want it too hot, the chillies should be deseeded before slicing, or for an even milder dish, sweet green peppers, deseeded and diced, can be used.

Lamb Steaks with Yoghurt, Cucumber and Mint (see page 52) *and Chicken and Mango Casserole* (see page 45) *with Fragrant Rice* (see page 99)

SPICED LIVER

For 4 people
Preparation time 20 minutes
Cooking time 15–20 minutes

450 g/1 lb liver, cut into thin slices
3 tablespoons vegetable oil
1 medium onion, chopped
1 clove garlic, crushed
1 teaspoon chilli powder
½ teaspoon ground coriander
grated rind of 1 lemon
1 teaspoon ground ginger
½ teaspoon turmeric
1 bay leaf
175 ml/6 fl oz thick coconut milk (see page 105)
2 teaspoons soft brown sugar
salt

All Indonesians love offal, so this fairly inexpensive commodity in Europe has a high price tag in Indonesia. Calves' liver is the best type to use for this dish, but lambs' or chickens' liver can be used equally as well without a great loss of taste.

1 Heat the oil in a wide, shallow pan and sauté the onion and garlic for 2 or 3 minutes.
2 Add the chilli powder, coriander, lemon rind, ginger, turmeric and bay leaf, mix well and stir for a few minutes on a low heat.
3 Add the liver and sauté on a high heat until the pinkness has gone, about 3–4 minutes.
4 Pour on the coconut milk, add the sugar and bring to the boil.
5 Reduce the heat to low and simmer for 5 minutes or until the liquid has thickened slightly.
6 Add salt to taste. Serve at once with rice and strips of plain omelette.

COOKED BEEF IN SOY SAUCE

For 4 people
Preparation time 30 minutes
Cooking time 20 minutes

1 kg/2 lb roast or boiled beef, thinly sliced
2 tablespoons vegetable oil
75 g/3 oz onions, diced
2 cloves garlic, crushed
½ whole nutmeg, grated
½ teaspoon black pepper
2 whole cloves
1 large potato, peeled and thinly sliced
1 tablespoon brown sugar
1 large tomato, chopped
2 tablespoons soy sauce
1 tablespoon lemon juice
2 hard-boiled eggs, peeled and halved
55 ml/2 fl oz water
4 spring onions, chopped

Any roast or boiled beef may be used for this recipe, which is known as Semur, *and it is always good for the leftovers of the Sunday roast.*

1 Heat the oil and gently fry the onions, garlic, nutmeg, black pepper and cloves until the onions are soft.
2 Add the meat and sliced potato and sauté for 1 minute.
3 Add the brown sugar, chopped tomato, soy sauce and lemon juice, mix well and cook gently for 5 minutes. Taste and add salt if necessary.
4 Add the hard-boiled eggs and water, cover and simmer for 5 more minutes.
5 Add the spring onions, if used, and serve immediately.

Note: You can, of course, make *Semur* with uncooked meat. It should be added at step 2 and cooked for a few minutes before the potato is added, then the whole dish will need to be cooked a little longer before serving.

If you follow the same recipe, leaving out the soy sauce and adding 1 tablespoon of ground chilli and a little more water at step 3, you will then have *Beef Madure*.

CHINESE-STYLE STEAK

For 4–6 people
Preparation time 20 minutes
Marinating time overnight
Cooking time 15 minutes

1 kg/2 lb fillet of beef

For the marinade
½ teaspoon salt
2 teaspoons sugar
1 tablespoon soy sauce
2 tablespoons cornflour
175 ml/6 fl oz water
55 ml/2 fl oz vegetable oil
1 egg, lightly beaten
55 ml/2 fl oz Worcestershire sauce

For the sauce
275 ml/½ pint beef stock (see page 9)
½ teaspoon salt
25 g/1 oz sugar
55 ml/2 fl oz Worcestershire sauce
3 teaspoons tomato sauce
1 teaspoon sesame oil (see page 125)

1 Slice the beef into 8 or 12 pieces.
2 Mix all the ingredients for the marinade together in a bowl and marinate the meat in the mixture overnight.
3 The next day, drain the meat and seal both sides in a hot deep frying pan. Remove and set aside in a warm place. Discard the marinade.
4 Combine all the ingredients for the sauce in the frying pan and mix well. Bring to the boil, stirring continuously, then turn the heat to low and simmer for 5 minutes.
5 Put in the beef fillet, cover the pan and continue simmering for 5 minutes. Check the seasoning and serve in a deep serving dish.
Note: You can use cheaper cuts of meat in place of the beef fillet, but naturally the cooking will take considerably longer. This is perfectly satisfactory as long as you remember to add a little water from time to time until the beef is cooked, as the lengthened cooking time will make the sauce very thick and liable to burn.

CRISP FRIED BEEF WITH COCONUT

For 2–4 people
Preparation time 20 minutes
Cooking time approximately 1 hour

There is no literal translation of this dish known as Dendeng Ragi *in Sumatra, but it is a 'dry', crisp, fried beef dish cooked with coconut.*

450 g/1 lb topside of beef, sliced thinly and cut into squares
50 g/2 oz onions, diced
3 cloves garlic, crushed
1 teaspoon chilli powder
1 teaspoon ground coriander
½ teaspoon ground cumin
10 whole black peppercorns, crushed
4 tablespoons white wine vinegar
1 teaspoon brown sugar
570 ml/1 pint water
salt to taste
225 g/8 oz desiccated coconut
5 tablespoons oil, preferably coconut or peanut

1 Put all the ingredients except the coconut and oil into a deep pan. Cover, bring to the boil and simmer for 40 minutes.
2 Add the coconut, stir well and taste, adding a little more salt if required.
3 Let the mixture cook gently until all the liquid has been absorbed by the coconut, then stir continuously until dry.
4 Add the oil and continue cooking and stirring until the coconut becomes a golden brown. Remove from the heat and serve hot or cold.

BEEF WITH DRY CHILLI PEPPER SAUCE

For 4 people
Preparation time 30 minutes
Cooking time 3–4 hours

This dish, known as Rendang, *is famous in Sumatra, especially around the west-central region known as Minangkabau. The original recipe calls for buffalo meat, which, though delicious, is as tough as old boots.* Rendang *can be cooked for a very long time and, better still, can be kept in a refrigerator for up to 2 weeks without spoiling. Even though it contains coconut milk, the long cooking process eventually turns this into oil, which acts as a form of preservative.*

Stir-fried Beef (see page 61) *with Yellow Rice* (see page 94) *and Semarang Beef* (see page 60) *with Plain Boiled Rice* (see page 94)

1 kg/2 lb good stewing steak, cut into large cubes
1 onion, diced
2 cloves garlic
1 teaspoon ground ginger
1 teaspoon turmeric
1 tablespoon chilli powder
1.7 litres/3 pints thick coconut milk (see page 105)
1 bay leaf
salt

1 Put the onion, garlic, ginger, turmeric and chilli powder into a blender and purée the ingredients, adding a little coconut milk.
2 Bring the remaining coconut milk, together with the puréed onion and garlic mixture, to the boil in a saucepan and add the beef cubes and bay leaf.
3 Bring back to the boil, turn down the heat and simmer gently, stirring occasionally, until it becomes very thick, about 1½–2 hours. Check for seasoning and add salt if required.
4 The slow cooking must now continue, and the meat and sauce must be stirred continuously until the meat absorbs all of the sauce and becomes golden brown in appearance. This process will take anything from 30 minutes to 1½ hours and requires persistence and patience.
5 Serve with plain boiled rice.

SEMARANG BEEF

For 4 people
Preparation time 30 minutes
Marinating time 1 hour
Cooking time 30 minutes

Semarang is a province on the island of Java, which lies between Bali and Sumatra. This style of cooking is often used in Europe, although the flavour of this dish is unique. Lapis Danging Semarang *is the local name for this dish, meaning 'layered beef'.*

1 kg/2 lb rump steak
175 g/6 oz onions, finely diced
2 cloves garlic, crushed
20 black peppercorns, crushed
a good pinch of nutmeg
4 tablespoons brown sugar
6 tablespoons soy sauce
50 g/2 oz unsalted butter
350 g/12 oz ripe tomatoes, peeled and chopped
salt

1 Slice the beef into small cutlets, and beat them out thinly with a cutlet bat or other flat object.
2 Make a marinade by mixing 110 g/4 oz diced onions with the garlic, peppercorns, nutmeg, sugar and soy sauce and place the slices of beef in it for 1 hour.
3 Heat the butter in a large frying pan and quickly sauté the beef slices for 1 minute on each side. Remove and set aside in a warm oven.
4 Add the remaining onions to the pan and fry gently until soft, about 3–5 minutes. Add the marinade and tomatoes, bring to the boil and simmer until the sauce becomes quite thick.
5 Season with salt, add the beef slices, heat through and serve immediately with plain boiled rice and salad.

Note: As I have mentioned before, the Indonesians seldom have the luxury of beef as we know it; their meat, usually buffalo, is tough and needs long cooking. If you choose to use a cheaper cut of meat, then the cooking time and method alters slightly. Add the meat to the pan with the marinade at step 3, stir-fry for a minute or so, then add the tomatoes and a little water. Simmer gently until the meat is tender. During this process, a little more water can be added with a whole stick of cinnamon and 2–4 cloves and salt to taste to add to the flavour.

STIR-FRIED BEEF

For 4–6 people
Preparation time 10 minutes
Marinating time 30 minutes
Cooking time 10 minutes

Variations of this can be found from the most northern point of China to the most southern point of Indonesia. Everywhere I have travelled, I have been amazed by the different textures and tastes, but the basic cooking method was always the same.

700 g/1½ lb rump steak, cut into strips
3 tablespoons soy sauce
2 cloves garlic, crushed
2 teaspoons cornflour
1 teaspoon sugar
4 tablespoons vegetable oil
1 teaspoon ground ginger
225 g/8 oz celery, diced

1 Combine the soy sauce, garlic, cornflour and sugar in a shallow bowl and mix well.
2 Add the strips of beef and make sure all the pieces are well coated. Cover and set aside for 30 minutes, stirring once or twice.
3 Heat the oil in a large frying pan, sprinkle on the ginger and add the beef mixture and stir-fry for 5 minutes.
4 Add the celery, stir-fry for a further 4 minutes and then serve immediately with plain boiled or yellow rice and a green salad.

STRIPS OF BEEF WITH CURRY SAUCE

For 6 people
Preparation time 20 minutes
Cooking time 40 minutes

This is a simple and very tasty way of making a curry that doesn't involve a lengthy cooking process.

450 g/1 lb loin of beef, cut into strips
salt
25 g/1 oz butter
25 g/1 oz onions, finely chopped
a thin slice of fresh ginger, cut into strips
25 g/1 oz curry powder, made into a paste with water
425 ml/¾ pint beef stock (see page 9)
110 g/4 oz potatoes, peeled and cut into matchsticks
4 tomatoes, skinned, deseeded and diced
55 ml/2 fl oz double cream, mixed with ½ teaspoon cornflour

1 Season the meat with salt.
2 Heat the butter in a saucepan and quickly brown the meat. Remove from the pan and set aside.
3 Add the onions to the pan and cook gently until soft.
4 Add the ginger and the curry paste and cook, stirring, for a few seconds.
5 Pour in the stock and simmer for 25 minutes.
6 Add the potatoes and cook until they are soft, then add the tomatoes.
7 Blend in the cream and cornflour mixture.
8 Return the beef to the pan, adjust seasoning and serve immediately.
Note: It is important not to overcook the beef or the potatoes, so there is a nice texture to the dish.

FILLET OF BEEF IN COCONUT CREAM

For 4 people
Preparation time 20 minutes
Cooking time 40 minutes

Sri Lanka, previously known as Ceylon, has the world's most colourful cuisine. Like so much of Southeast Asia, the visiting Dutch, Indian, Malay, English and Portuguese visitors have left behind their own recipes, spices and cooking techniques to an already varied cuisine. Curries are the centre of most meals and come in all flavours and colours: white curries, mild and creamy, with cream and milk; red curries, bright scarlet from pounded dried chillies; and curries as black as night.

550 g/1¼ lb fillet of beef in one piece
salt and pepper
10 g/½ oz coriander
10 g/½ oz cumin
½ teaspoon fenugreek seeds
1 large onion
4 cloves garlic
40 g/1½ oz unsalted butter
5-cm/2-inch stick cinnamon
½ teaspoon turmeric
1 teaspoon chilli powder
3 bay leaves
30 ml/1 fl oz white wine vinegar
110 ml/4 fl oz beef stock (see page 9)
110 ml/4 fl oz thick coconut milk (see page 105)
fresh coriander leaves or parsley to garnish (optional)

1 Trim the beef of any excess fat or sinews. Tie securely with kitchen string every 5–7.5 cm/2–3 inches and season with salt and pepper.
2 Toast the coriander, cumin and fenugreek under a grill or in a dry saucepan for 2 minutes and then grind to a fine powder.
3 Finely chop the onion and garlic.
4 Heat the butter in a frying pan large enough to hold the beef and seal all sides of the beef. Transfer to a roasting dish and place in a hot oven, 200°C/400°F/Gas Mark 6, for 10–15 minutes, depending upon how well you like it cooked.
5 Fry the onion and garlic in the pan you sealed the beef in until lightly browned
6 Add the cinnamon and the ground spices, turmeric, chilli powder, bay leaves and wine vinegar and stir well.
7 Add the beef stock and simmer, scraping up and blending all the meat deposits and spices. Reduce until the liquid has almost evaporated.
8 Add the coconut milk and blend in well.
9 Strain through a fine sieve into a clean pan and season with salt. Replace on a gentle heat.
10 Remove the meat from the oven and slice finely, discarding the string.
11 Arrange the sliced beef attractively on plates and spoon the sauce carefully around it. Serve immediately, garnished with fresh coriander leaves or parsley.
Note: If your coconut milk is not thick enough, you may add a ¼ teaspoon of arrowroot or cornflour to it before adding to the sauce. Alternatively, dilute the arrowroot or cornflour in a little water and add it a little at a time at the end of cooking, so that you can see the sauce thickening to suit your requirements. The onions, garlic and chilli powder can be doubled if desired.

Fillet of Beef in Coconut Cream, Indonesian Spaghetti (see page 92) *and Spiced Fried Leeks* (see page 92)

GOLDEN PORK

For 4–6 people
Preparation time 15 minutes
Cooking time 2 hours

Some say this dish originated in Burma and I must admit the extensive use of garlic and ginger reflects Burmese tastes. Then again, I ate a similar dish in Paris, cooked by a Frenchman who claimed it to be French provincial cooking!

1 kg/2 lb lean pork, cut into cubes
450 g/1 lb onions, finely diced
9 cloves garlic, crushed
150 g/5 oz fresh ginger, peeled and finely chopped
2 tablespoons water
2 tablespoons vinegar
55 ml/2 fl oz vegetable oil
½ teaspoon chilli powder
½ teaspoon sugar
salt

1 Put the onions, garlic, ginger and water into a blender and blend to a smooth paste.
2 Place a clean cloth over a saucepan and pour the contents of the blender into the cloth and squeeze gently to extract as much liquid as possible into the saucepan.
3 Add the pork, vinegar, vegetable oil, chilli powder, sugar and salt and bring to the boil, stirring well to mix all the ingredients thoroughly.
4 Cover, reduce the heat to low and simmer gently for up to 2 hours or until the pork is tender. (If the mixture becomes too dry during cooking, add a tablespoon of water.) The finished appearance of this dish should be as the name suggests, 'golden'.

SPICED ROAST PORK

For 4–6 people
Preparation time 20 minutes
Cooking time 1 hour 30 minutes

This is a really good variation to the traditional roast pork served for Sunday lunch in England.

1 kg/2 lb loin of pork (skin left on)
2 tablespoons roasted coriander
½ teaspoon whole black peppercorns
5 mm/¼ inch stick cinnamon
1 large onion, quartered
2 cloves garlic, crushed
30 ml/1 fl oz soy sauce
2 teaspoons sugar
salt
a little vinegar

1 Grind the coriander, peppercorns and cinnamon to a fine powder.
2 Purée the onion and, using only 110 g/4 oz, mix it with the ground spices and garlic to make a paste.
4 Add the soy sauce, sugar and a little salt to the spice mixture, and mix together well.
5 Rub this mixture all over the underside of the pork, working it in well with your fingers.
6 Place the pork in a greased roasting pan with the skin side uppermost and brush the skin with vinegar.
7 Place in a hot oven, 200°C/400°F/Gas Mark 6, for 20 minutes, then reduce the heat to 180°C/350°F/Gas Mark 4 and cook for 1 hour or until the pork is cooked.

8 Remove from the oven, cut into slices and serve.

Note: The amount of fat and liquid in pork will always vary. Cooking times will therefore depend upon the actual piece of meat. A piece of meat weighing 1 kg/2 lb and 15 cm/6 inches thick will take longer to cook than a similar joint of the same weight but only 7.5 cm/3 inches thick. So keep an eye on the joint at all times.

You can make a delicious sauce or gravy from the residue in the pan, to serve with the pork.

Worcestershire sauce may be used in place of soy sauce.

SPICED ROAST PORK 2

For 2–4 people
Preparation time 10 minutes
Cooking time 15 minutes

This is a good remedy for any leftover roast pork. It transforms it into something totally different.

450 g/1 lb cooked pork, cut into pieces
2 tablespoons roasted coriander
½ teaspoon whole black peppercorns
5 mm/¼ inch stick cinnamon
1 large onion, quartered
1 clove garlic, crushed
1 tablespoon vegetable oil
½ teaspoon soy sauce, mixed with 1 tablespoon water
½ teaspoon sugar
salt

1 Grind the coriander, peppercorns and cinnamon to a fine powder.

2 Purée the onion and, using only 110 g/4 oz, mix with the garlic.

3 Heat the oil in a pan, add the garlic and onion paste, fry for a few minutes, then add the spices. Stir well and fry for a few minutes more.

4 Add the soy sauce and sugar and blend in well.

5 Add the pork pieces, mixing well in so that all the pork is coated. Season with salt.

6 Transfer to a roasting pan and heat through in a warm oven, 150°C/300°F/Gas Mark 2, for 10–15 minutes.

Note: Worcestershire sauce can replace the soy sauce, but add a little more sugar.

SWEET PORK

For 3–4 people
Preparation time 20 minutes
Cooking time 25 minutes

700 g/1½ lb belly of pork, thinly sliced
2 teaspoons salt
1 teaspoon ground black pepper
50 g/2 oz plain flour
oil for deep-frying
225 g/8 oz onions, diced
2 cloves garlic, crushed
1 tablespoon tomato purée
55 ml/2 fl oz chicken stock
25 g/1 oz brown sugar
55 ml/2 fl oz sweet soy sauce
chopped parsley to garnish

1 Sprinkle the pork with salt and pepper, dust with flour and set aside for 10 minutes.
2 Heat the oil to smoking point, carefully drop in the pork and fry until well browned. Remove from oil and set aside on absorbent paper towel.
3 Put 2 tablespoons of the hot oil used to fry the pork in a large frying pan and fry the onions and garlic for 3 minutes.
4 Stir in the tomato purée, chicken stock, brown sugar and the fried pork slices. Mix together well, sprinkle on the soy sauce, bring to the boil and simmer for 10 minutes. If the liquid should evaporate too quickly, just add a little more water.
5 Turn up the heat and cook for a further 6–8 minutes or until all the liquid is absorbed into the pork and it is very tender.
6 Serve at once, sprinkled with chopped parsley.

BALINESE PORK

For 4 people
Preparation time 20 minutes
Cooking time 45 minutes

1 kg/2 lb lean pork, cut into thin strips
55 ml/2 fl oz vegetable oil
4 cloves garlic, crushed
½ teaspoon ground ginger
1 medium onion or 4 spring onions, diced
½ teaspoon chilli powder
2 teaspoons brown sugar
2 tablespoons soy sauce
450 g/1 lb tomatoes, chopped
1 tablespoon lemon juice
50 g/2 oz green pepper, cut into fine strips
salt
275 ml/½ pint water
110 g/4 oz mushrooms, sliced

Danging Masak Bali, *as the Balinese call this dish, is typical of the flavour of this heavenly island.*

1 Heat the oil and fry the pieces of pork until they change colour. If you haven't a large enough pan, this can be done in two or three lots. Remove from the pan and set aside.
2 Add the garlic, ginger and onion, if used, to the pan and fry gently for 2–3 minutes.
3 Return the meat to the pan, add the chilli powder, sugar, soy sauce, tomatoes, lemon juice, green pepper, a little salt and the water and mix well. Cover and simmer gently for 20 minutes.
4 Add the mushrooms and spring onions, if used, and stir well. Cover and simmer for 10 minutes more, by which time the meat will be tender and the gravy thick. If the gravy does dry out, quickly add more water.
5 Taste and add more salt if necessary. Serve with plain boiled rice.
Note: Fresh chillies and ginger should be used in this dish if available. A 2.5-cm/1-inch piece of ginger, crushed, should be added at step 2, and 3 green chillies, seeds removed and diced, should be added at the beginning of step 4.

Beef may be substituted for the pork.

Glazed Pork Spareribs (see page 69), *Indonesian Fried Noodles* (see page 72) *and Vegetable Curry* (see page 89)

SWEET MINCE

For 4 people
Preparation time 20 minutes
Cooking time 25 minutes

225 g/8 oz lean pork, minced
275 ml/½ pint coconut milk (see page 105)
225 g/8 oz prawns, cooked and minced
1 teaspoon salt
2 teaspoons sugar
1 red chilli, seeds removed and finely sliced
freshly ground black pepper
parsley to garnish

This unusual combination of ingredients is very typical of Javanese cuisine which, oddly enough, is very similar to the cuisine of Thailand. This makes a delicious light luncheon dish, which I would serve with potato crisps.

1 Put the coconut milk into a saucepan, bring to the boil, then simmer for 5 minutes.
2 Add the minced pork and cook for 15 minutes.
3 Put in the prawns, season with salt, sugar, chilli and pepper and simmer for 2–3 minutes.
4 Pour into a deep serving dish and garnish with parsley.

SWEET AND SOUR SPARERIBS

For 4 people
Preparation time 20 minutes
Cooking time approximately 2 hours

1 kg/2 lb spareribs
30 ml/1 fl oz vegetable oil
2 cloves garlic, crushed
5-cm/2-inch piece fresh ginger, peeled and chopped
1 medium green pepper, seeds and pith removed, diced
1 medium red pepper, seeds and pith removed, diced
175 g/6 oz can pineapple, cut into chunks and juice reserved
30 ml/1 fl oz white wine vinegar
30 ml/1 fl oz soy sauce
25 g/1 oz soft brown sugar
salt and pepper
½ tablespoon cornflour mixed with 2 tablespoons water

I have yet to come across two identical recipes or even taste similar flavours in the battle for the supremacy of the sparerib.

1 Preheat the oven to 220°C/425°F/Gas Mark 7. Place the spareribs in a roasting pan, cover with foil and roast for 30 minutes.
2 Meanwhile, heat the oil in a large frying pan and sauté the garlic and ginger for 1 minute.
3 Add the peppers and fry for 5 minutes, stirring occasionally. Stir in the pineapple and continue to cook for 3 minutes.
4 Add the reserved pineapple juice, wine vinegar, soy sauce, sugar and salt and pepper and bring to the boil.
5 Remove the spareribs from the oven and pour off the fat. Turn the oven temperature down to 180°C/350°F/Gas Mark 4.
6 Pour the boiling sauce over the spareribs and make sure the ribs are well coated with the mixture. Return them to the oven and cook for 1 hour, basting occasionally.
7 Remove from the oven and transfer the ribs only to a serving dish.
8 Put the roasting pan over a gentle heat, stir in the cornflour mixture and cook until the sauce thickens, stirring continuously.
9 Pour the sauce over the ribs and serve immediately.

Note: If fresh root ginger is not available, use 1 teaspoon ground ginger and 50 g/2 oz finely diced onions, adding the onions at step 2 and the ground ginger at the end of step 3.

GLAZED PORK SPARERIBS

For 4 people
Preparation time 20 minutes
Cooking time 1 hour 30 minutes

No Eastern cookery book is complete without some reference to pork spare-ribs. Although there does not seem to be any graceful way of serving them, I am sure the taste of this particular dish will more than compensate for its unelegant appearance.

1 kg/2 lb pork spareribs
110 ml/4 fl oz liquid honey
110 ml/4 fl oz tomato ketchup
110 g/4 oz onions, chopped
2 cloves garlic, peeled and crushed
rind of 1 orange
juice of ½ orange
1 tablespoon vinegar
1 tablespoon olive oil
1 teaspoon strong Dijon mustard
¼ teaspoon salt
¼ teaspoon freshly ground pepper
1 teaspoon Worcestershire sauce
2 or 3 drops Tabasco sauce
3 cloves

1 Preheat the oven to 180°C/350°F/Gas Mark 4.
2 Place the spareribs in a roasting dish, cover with foil and roast for 30 minutes.
3 While the ribs are cooking, combine all the remaining ingredients in a suitable pan and bring to the boil. Reduce the heat and simmer gently for 5 minutes.
4 Remove the roasting dish from the oven and drain off all the liquid. Increase the heat of the oven to 200°C/400°F/Gas Mark 6.
5 Pour the sauce over the spareribs making sure all the ribs are coated.
6 Place in the oven and roast for 1 hour, basting occasionally.

Note: This sauce can be used with any fish, meat or poultry, roasted or grilled. I generally make up large portions of this sauce and store it in the refrigerator. When friends drop in (generally after midnight!), I can then quickly heat this sauce with some cold cooked meat or fresh fish, throw together a salad, and I have a delicious supper prepared in minutes, which goes a long way to enhancing my reputation as a wizard in the kitchen. Little do they know!

PORK SATAY

For 4 people
Preparation time 30 minutes
Marinating time 2 hours
Cooking time 30 minutes

The smell of barbecued satay *is as integral a part of Indonesian life as the smell of roast beef on Sunday is to the Englishman. However, recipes will vary from household to household and this one was a favourite of an old aunt of mine.*

450 g/1 lb lean pork, trimmed of excess fat and cut into cubes
2 cloves garlic, crushed
½ teaspoon ground ginger
2 teaspoons honey
¼ teaspoon ground fennel
½ teaspoon ground cinnamon
¼ teaspoon ground black pepper
¼ teaspoon chilli powder
2 tablespoons soy sauce
a pinch of ground cloves
a little vegetable oil

1 Mix together the garlic, ginger, honey, fennel, cinnamon, pepper, chilli, soy sauce and cloves in a deep bowl.
2 Add the pork cubes to this marinade, mix everything together well and set aside for 2 hours.
3 Preheat the oven to 190°C/375°F/Gas Mark 5.
4 Thread the pork cubes onto four skewers.
5 Line a baking tray with foil, brush it with oil and lay the skewered pork on it. Place in the oven for 25–30 minutes, turning once halfway through the cooking.
6 Serve immediately with wedges of lime or lemon, celery sticks and cucumber slices.
Note: This recipe will take on a new flavour if you can take the trouble to find fennel seeds, whole black peppercorns, cinnamon, fresh chilli and fresh green ginger, and grind and crush these ingredients to make your marinade. Adding more or less of any ingredient will add your own personality to this recipe and will not detract from this popular dish.

MALAYSIAN PORK CHOPS

For 4 people
Preparation time 15 minutes
Marinating time 30 minutes
Cooking time 30 minutes

4 pork chops
1 tablespoon coriander seeds
12 black peppercorns, crushed
3 tablespoon soy sauce
1 teaspoon soft brown sugar
a pinch of salt

1 Gently toast the coriander seeds in a dry frying pan until they change colour. Lay the seeds on a clean work surface and crush them coarsely with a rolling pin. (Place the seeds inside a polythene bag, as it makes less mess.)
2 Mix the crushed coriander seeds, peppercorns, soy sauce and soft brown sugar together in a shallow dish.
3 Lightly sprinkle a little salt over the chops, put into the dish and coat well with the mixture. Cover and set aside for 30 minutes, basting occasionally.
4 Preheat the grill to high. Place the chops on a rack in the grill pan, place the grill pan as near as possible to the heat source and grill for 2 minutes each side.
5 Reduce the heat to moderate, lower the grill pan one rung and grill the chops 10 minutes on each side, basting frequently with the marinating liquid. Serve at once.
Note: Another method of cooking this dish is to seal both sides of the chops in a hot frying pan with a little oil and then to transfer them to a moderate oven, 350°F/180°C/Gas Mark 4, for 15 minutes, basting frequently. The reason I recommend roasting the coriander seeds is to enhance that warm, faintly orangey fragrance, which to me is the basis of all homemade curry-type dishes.

Sunset Fish (see page 34) *and Steamed Fish with Coconut and Sesame* (see page 33)

INDONESIAN FRIED NOODLES

For 4 people
Preparation time 10 minutes
Cooking time 20 minutes

225 g/8 oz egg noodles (vermicelli)
4 tablespoons vegetable oil
1 medium onion, finely chopped
2 cloves garlic, crushed
½ teaspoon ground ginger
1 teaspoon chilli or chilli sauce (optional)
75 g/3 oz pork fillet, cut into small pieces
50 g/2 oz frozen prawns, thawed
1 large celery stalk, chopped
2 medium carrots, peeled and diced
2 white cabbage leaves, shredded
2 tomatoes, skinned, deseeded and chopped
2 tablespoons soy sauce
4 spring onions, chopped
salt and pepper
a little chopped parsley

Noodles, which in Indonesia are called bahmi, *are traditionally a Chinese dish. The Dutch are extremely fond of noodles and in Holland they appear in a myriad of variations. Here is an example of an integration of styles, with a dish of Chinese origin developed for European tastes by a Javanese cook.*

1 Cook the noodles in boiling, salted water for 3–5 minutes (or according to the instructions on the packet). Drain into a colander and rinse under cold running water, then set aside.
2 Heat the oil in a large deep-frying pan, add the onion, garlic, ginger and chilli, if used, and stir-fry for 3 minutes.
3 Add the pork and prawns and continue to stir-fry for 2 minutes.
4 Stir in the celery, carrots and cabbage and fry for another 4 minutes.
5 Add the noodles and continue cooking, stirring, for 3 minutes. Add the tomatoes, soy sauce and spring onions, season to taste with salt and pepper and keep stir-frying until the noodles are really hot.
6 Garnish with parsley and serve immediately.

Note: This dish is versatile in that the pork can be changed for beef or chicken, or even game, if desired.

It may also be made into a soup by adding 850 ml/1½ pints of beef or chicken stock at the end of step 4, bringing it to the boil and then continuing as before.

Vegetables

Those who live in the Western world have difficulty in appreciating how important vegetables are in the diet of those who live in the tropics. It is quite common for one of the tuber family to be the staple food of a community – that is the crop which supplies the starch or sugar on which the people depend for their physical survival. It is accepted that in vast areas this carbohydrate is supplied by rice or other grain. However, man cannot live on starch alone. He must have proteins, fats, salts and vitamins, and these are plentiful in green vegetables and seed crops, either grown in gardens or bought from the market. For this and for religious and economic reasons, vegetables play an important role not fully appreciated in the prosperous West.

It is quite common to find that some meals will consist entirely of vegetables, enhanced with spices, which may be cooked or uncooked, served simply by themselves or with fruit and creamy sauces. But in all cases, Eastern cooks have developed a finesse for cooking vegetables which requires a subtlety of touch for slow, gentle cooking, or to cook quickly to retain the crispness that is so evident in Chinese cooking. Whatever method or recipe is used in this chapter, the overall emphasis must be to select your vegetables carefully according to season or taste – nothing can enhance the appearance or flavour of tired vegetables.

SPICED VEGETABLE SALAD

For 4–6 people
Preparation time 30 minutes
Cooking time 25 minutes

1 cucumber
225 g/8 oz carrots
225 g/8 oz fine French beans
225 g/8 oz cauliflower
1 red pimento
10 small pickling onions
3 whole almonds
50 g/2 oz onions, diced
2 cloves garlic
2 tablespoons vegetable oil
½ teaspoon turmeric
½ teaspoon chilli powder
½ teaspoon ground ginger
4 tablespoons white wine vinegar
salt
2 teaspoons brown sugar
1 teaspoon dry English mustard

1 Wash and prepare all the vegetables. Peel the cucumber and carrots and cut into 1-cm/½-inch lengths, the thickness of matchsticks. Top and tail the fine French beans, which should all be the same size. (If the beans are large, slice them diagonally into three.) Break the cauliflower down into individual tiny florets. Core and discard the seeds and pith from the pimento and slice into fine strips. Peel the pickling onions. In the meantime, bring a pan of salted water to the boil.
2 Crush or pound the almonds, diced onions and garlic to a paste and sauté in the vegetable oil over a high heat for 1 minute. Add the turmeric, chilli powder, ground ginger and pickling onions. Stir well, then add the vinegar and a pinch of salt. Cover and cook for 2 minutes.
3 Plunge the carrots into the boiling water and, as soon as the water comes back to the boil again, remove the carrots and refresh them under cold running water. Do the same with the beans and the cauliflower.
4 Add the pimento and water used for cooking the vegetables to the pan containing the pickling onions, and cook, covered, for 5 minutes.
5 Add the sugar and dry mustard, stir well, then add the carrots, cauliflower, French beans and cucumber. Cover and cook for 3 minutes.
6 Serve immediately hot, or leave overnight to cool and serve chilled.

COOKED VEGETABLE SALAD

For 6–8 people
Preparation time 30 minutes
Cooking time 15 minutes

This is not in the truest sense a salad, as the vegetables are blanched first. These cooked salads are numerous in Indonesia, where they are always served chilled as part of the main meal. Any combination of vegetables may be used according to season or taste.

4 carrots, peeled and cut into matchsticks
175 g/6 oz French beans, topped and tailed
110 g/4 oz celery, diced
110 g/4 oz cauliflower florets
25 ml/1 fl oz vegetable oil
110 g/4 oz onions, diced
50 g/2 oz sesame seeds
salt

1 Bring a large pan of salted water to the boil.
2 Immerse the carrots in the boiling water for 1 minute, remove and refresh under cold water. Drain and set aside.
3 Repeat the process with the French beans, celery and cauliflower, but cook these for 2 minutes each.
4 Heat the oil in a frying pan on a gentle heat, then add the onions. Increase the heat to high and fry the onions until brown and slightly crisp. Remove the onions with a slotted spoon and drain on paper towel. Discard half the oil.

Cos Lettuce and Mango Salad (see page 77), *Cooked Vegetable Salad and Tiger Melon Salad with Prawns* (see page 80)

5 Arrange the vegetables on a suitable dish.
6 Heat a separate pan on a low heat and add the sesame seeds and gently toast the seeds until brown. Set aside.
7 Stir a pinch of salt into the reserved oil and spoon over the vegetables, followed by the fried onions and sesame seeds. Chill before serving.

VEGETABLE SALADS WITH COCONUT DRESSING

For 4 people
Preparation time 30 minutes
Cooking time 5 minutes

Vegetable salads, commonly known as urap, *have the unique distinction of either being eaten cooked or raw. Any combination of vegetables may be used, bearing in mind seasonal availability and freshness. The* bumbu, *or dressing, is also served hot or cold.*

Raw vegetable salad
75 g/3 oz carrots, peeled and cut into matchsticks
75 g/3 oz white cabbage, shredded
75 g/3 oz celery, diced
1 small bunch watercress
6 radishes, finely sliced
½ cucumber, finely sliced
2 spring onions, diced
a small handful of fresh mint leaves, chopped

1 Place all the ingredients for the dressing in a suitable pan, bring to the boil and simmer for 5 minutes, stirring continuously. Remove from the heat and allow to cool.
2 Take all the prepared raw vegetables and the mint and put them into a deep bowl. Sprinkle on the cold coconut dressing, toss well and serve.

Cooked vegetable salad
75 g/3 oz French beans, topped and tailed
75 g/3 oz cauliflower florets
75 g/3 oz broccoli heads
75 g/3 oz carrots, peeled and cut into matchsticks

1 Blanch each of the vegetables for not more than 2 minutes in boiling salted water, then run each under cold water to arrest the cooking process.
2 Make the coconut dressing as described previously but, after simmering for 5 minutes, add the cold blanched vegetables, mix well and allow to simmer for a minute or two before serving.
Note: Fresh grated coconut is obviously ideal for this recipe if you can get some. Substitute half of the grated white flesh of the fresh coconut for the desiccated coconut and milk. *Do not cook* the fresh coconut dressing, just mix all the ingredients together and add to the cold raw or hot cooked vegetables.

Coconut dressing
175 g/6 oz desiccated coconut
275 ml/½ pint milk
¼ teaspoon yeast extract or soy sauce
½ teaspoon chilli powder
1 clove garlic, crushed
a pinch of sugar
juice of ½ lime or lemon
salt to taste

SAVOURY SALAD

For 6 people
Preparation time 15 minutes

This is a very different and lovely way of serving a salad.

225 g/8 oz apples (Granny Smith), peeled, cored and diced
1 small pineapple, peeled, cored and diced
225 g/8 oz lean cooked pork, diced
110 g/4 oz cooked prawns, shelled
6 spring onions, chopped
50 g/2 oz celery, chopped
1 Cos lettuce, left whole, well washed and drained
1 small bunch watercress, stalks removed
50 g/2 oz flaked almonds, toasted

Dressing
75 ml/3 fl oz olive oil
juice of 1 lemon
30 ml/3 fl oz soy sauce
1 tablespoon soft brown sugar
salt and pepper

1 Whisk all the ingredients for the dressing in a small bowl and set aside.
2 Put the apples, pineapple, pork, prawns, spring onions and celery into a large bowl, pour over the dressing and mix well.
3 Trim away any unsightly leaves from the lettuce and cut out a cavity in the centre of the lettuce with a sharp knife. Slice across the base of the lettuce, so that it is able to stand upright. Shred the piece of lettuce cut from the cavity and arrange around the base. Arrange the watercress leaves on top of this.
4 Fill the cavity of the lettuce with the salad mixture and scatter over the flaked almonds. Serve at once, as it is.

COS LETTUCE AND MANGO SALAD

For 4 people
Preparation time 20 minutes
Marinating time 30 minutes

1 cos lettuce
1 bunch watercress
1 mango
5 tablespoons peanut oil
1 tablespoon lime or lemon juice
1 tablespoon French mustard
salt and pepper to taste
a pinch of sugar

1 Wash and dry the lettuce and watercress.
2 Cut the lettuce in half and slice the two halves very finely. Set aside.
3 Peel and slice the mango and cut into dice. Mix together the oil, lime or lemon juice, French mustard, salt, pepper and sugar and marinate the mango in this for 30 minutes.
4 Just before serving, add the lettuce and watercress and toss well.

SALAD EXOTIQUE

For 2 people
Preparation time 20 minutes
Cooking time 5 minutes

110 g/4 oz mange-tout (snow peas), topped and tailed
75 g/3 oz cucumber, thinly sliced
1 mango, peeled and sliced
6 nasturtium leaves
2 nasturtium flowers
French or Oriental dressing (see page 82)

1 Blanch the mange-tout in boiling salted water for 1 minute. Remove and immerse immediately in cold water.
2 Arrange the sliced cucumber on a plate with the mange-tout, mango, nasturtium leaves and flowers.
3 Sprinkle with French or Oriental dressing before serving.
Note: The bright yellow, orange or red flowers with round, flat leaves flourish from midsummer until the first frost. The buds, leaves and flowers add a sharp, peppery bite to salads.

LOBSTER SALAD

For 2 people
Preparation time 30 minutes
Cooking time 30 minutes

2 live lobsters, weighing 450 g/1 lb each
3 litres/5 pints boiling salted water
1 tablespoon olive oil
40 g/1½ oz shallots, peeled and finely diced
½ clove garlic, peeled and finely diced
110 ml/4 fl oz thick coconut milk (see page 105)
25 g/1 oz green pepper, seeds and pith removed and finely diced
75 g/3 oz apple, peeled and cored and finely diced
75 g/3 oz nibbed hazelnuts, roasted
1 tablespoon Worcestershire sauce
salt and ground pepper
a pinch of caster sugar
1 lettuce, washed and dried
2 large ripe tomatoes, peeled, deseeded and diced
2 thin slices fresh or canned pineapple, diced

1 Drop the lobsters into the boiling water and cook for 7 minutes. Drain and cool under cold running water.
2 Cut the shells open and extract the meat. Chop into small pieces.
3 Heat the oil in a small saucepan, add the shallots and garlic and sauté for 2 minutes over a low heat.
4 Pour in the coconut milk, simmer until it has reduced a little, then remove from the heat.
5 Add the diced green pepper, diced apple, nibbed hazelnuts and Worcestershire sauce. Mix well.
6 Season to taste with salt and pepper and sugar.
7 Arrange the lettuce on two plates, surround with tomato and pineapple pieces, arrange lobster meat in centre and pour on the sauce.
8 Serve slightly chilled.
Note: At step 7, the Worcestershire sauce can be replaced by a light soy sauce and the salad can be garnished with a fresh red chilli, thinly sliced, before serving.

Spiced Sautéed Potatoes (see page 84), *Indonesian Caviar* (see page 90) *and Dried Bean Curry* (see page 91)

TIGER MELON SALAD WITH PRAWNS

For 4 people
Preparation time 30 minutes

1 small round Tiger melon or Sugar Baby watermelon
16 large precooked Mediterranean prawns
freshly ground white pepper
salt

1 Cut the melon into quarters.
2 Separate the flesh from the rind with a sharp knife. Remove all the black seeds and cut into cubes.
3 Sprinkle with freshly ground white pepper and set aside.
4 Shell the prawns and remove the black intestinal tract by running a sharp knife down the back and rinsing under cold water.
5 Pat dry with kitchen paper towel, season and set aside.
6 Place peppered watermelon cubes attractively on a plate. Set 4 prawns per person on top.
7 Spoon the sauce (below) onto the side of each plate and garnish with slices of cucumber, a nasturtium leaf and a twist of lime.

TARRAGON TOMATO SAUCE

350 g/12 oz ripe tomatoes
3 tablespoons double cream
1 tablespoon strong Dijon mustard
2 tablespoons white wine vinegar
10 fresh tarragon leaves, or 15 tarragon leaves preserved in white vinegar
1 tablespoon freshly chopped parsley
salt and cayenne pepper or Tabasco to taste

1 Skin and deseed the tomatoes, chop to a fine purée and put to drain in a fine-meshed sieve. Discard the juice.
2 Put the cream into a bowl, add the mustard and whisk them together. Gradually pour in the wine vinegar, whisking all the time. Finally, mix in the drained tomatoes, herbs, salt and cayenne pepper or Tabasco to taste. Keep in a cool place.

FRUIT AND VEGETABLE SALAD

For 4 people
Preparation time 30 minutes
Marinating time 1 hour

This salad has a definite Western touch about it in the mixture of fruit and vegetables. It has a clean, sharp taste, and can be eaten with the main course or, in the Continental fashion, after the main course.

1 Mix all the ingredients for the dressing together thoroughly.
2 Put all the prepared vegetable ingredients into a deep bowl, pour on the dressing and toss well. Set aside for 1 hour, tossing occasionally, before serving.

50 g/2 oz celery, diced
110 g/4 oz white cabbage, shredded
½ cucumber, cut in half lengthways, deseeded and sliced
2 firm eating apples, peeled, cored and finely sliced
6 radishes, finely sliced
2 carrots, peeled and cut into matchsticks

Dressing
30 ml/1 fl oz white wine vinegar
1 teaspoon caster sugar
2 teaspoons salt
a pinch of cayenne pepper
1 tablespoon water

CUCUMBER AND YOGHURT SALAD

For 4 people
Preparation time 30 minutes
Marinating time 1 hour

This salad, known as Raita, *is a natural accompaniment to hot, spicy dishes, or a refreshing starter on a hot day.*

1 Wash and dice the cucumber, sprinkle with salt and set aside to drain for 30 minutes.
2 Beat the yoghurt until it is smooth and add the spring onion.
3 Squeeze the cucumber to extract as much liquid as possible, and add to the yoghurt. Season to taste with salt and pepper and a little sugar.
4 Spoon into a serving bowl, cover and refrigerate for at least 1 hour.
5 Arrange the lettuce on individual plates, spoon on the salad mixture and sprinkle a little paprika on top.
Note: As an alternative, a heaped tablespoon of chopped fresh mint can be added to the above to 'heighten' the flavour.

½ cucumber
salt, pepper and a little caster sugar to taste
275 ml/½ pint natural yoghurt
1 spring onion, finely chopped
1 crisp lettuce, cut into 4
a little paprika to garnish

ONION SALAD

For 4–6 people
Preparation time 1 hour 10 minutes

225 g/8 oz onions, finely sliced
1 tablespoon salt
2 tablespoons pale muscavado sugar
55 ml/2 fl oz lemon juice
4 ripe tomatoes, peeled, deseeded and diced
1 tablespoon fine shreds of fresh ginger
3 fresh green or red chillies, sliced (see note)
salt to taste
2 tablespoons chopped parsley

1 Sprinkle the onions with salt and set aside for 1 hour, then squeeze out all the liquid and rinse once in cold water. Drain.
2 Dissolve the sugar in the lemon juice, mix all the ingredients together in a glass bowl, chill and serve.
Note: You can adjust the heat of this recipe by adding more or less chillies. For less heat, the chillies can be deseeded and sliced, or can be substituted wholly or partly by green or red sweet peppers.

VINAIGRETTE DRESSINGS

The simplest of all cold sauces is a vinaigrette, usually made with five parts of oil to one of wine vinegar and seasoned with a small squeeze of lemon juice, salt and pepper and a pinch of sugar.

French Dressing
Add to the above 1 teaspoon strong Dijon mustard.

Oriental Dressing
1 tablespoon light soy sauce
2 tablespoons safflower or sunflower oil
1 teaspoon shredded fresh ginger or 2 tablespoons green ginger wine
squeeze of lemon juice
a pinch of sugar
1 tablespoon sesame oil

1 Blend all the ingredients except the sesame oil together.
2 Add the sesame oil a little at a time to taste, as different brands vary in strength.
Note: Safflower oil and sunflower oil, because they are light, mild and thinly textured, are ideal for mixing with more expensive oils for delicate dishes such as salads.

COLD SAUCES FOR SALADS

Recipe 1
Mix all the ingredients together.
Recipe 2
To the above, add 1 tablespoon of mango chutney, making sure that the pieces of mango are finely chopped
Recipe 3
Add 1 tablespoon toasted, ground sesame seeds to either recipe 1 or 2. Or, if you are feeling adventurous, try mixing all three together.

This is a wonderful accompaniment for any cold meal or salad. Try the sauce on slices of fresh pineapple.

30 ml/1 fl oz chilli sauce
50 g/2 oz peanut butter
30 ml/1 fl oz white wine vinegar
75 ml/3 fl oz cold water
3 teaspoons caster sugar (according to taste)
salt to taste

SAVOURY POTATOES

For 4 people
Preparation time 20 minutes
Cooking time 30 minutes

1 Heat the butter or oil in a saucepan and sauté the mustard seeds until they start to pop.
2 Add the onions and continue to cook for 5 minutes on a low heat.
3 Add the turmeric and chilli powder, stir, then put in the diced potatoes, sprinkle with salt and toss gently to mix everything together. Serve hot or cold.

450 g/1 lb potatoes, peeled, boiled and diced
25 g/1 oz butter or oil
¼ teaspoon black mustard seeds
225 g/8 oz onions, diced
½ teaspoon turmeric
½ teaspoon chilli powder
1 teaspoon salt

SPICED POTATO SLICES

For 4 people
Preparation time 25 minutes
Cooking time 15–20 minutes

1 Thoroughly wash the potatoes and cook them in their skins until cooked but firm, testing regularly to make sure they are not overcooked. Drain, cool and cut into slices.
2 Sift together the salt, cumin, chilli, mixed spices and caster sugar two or three times to blend thoroughly, then sprinkle over the potato slices.
3 Add the lemon juice and toss gently to combine all the flavours.
4 Serve as a snack on its own, as a side dish, or as part of a buffet.

450 g/1 lb small new potatoes
1 teaspoon salt
1 teaspoon ground cumin
½ teaspoon chilli powder
½ teaspoon mixed spices (see page 106)
½ teaspoon caster sugar
1 teaspoon lemon juice

CREAMED SPICED POTATOES

For 4 people
Preparation time 20 minutes
Cooking time 20 minutes

225 g/8 oz potatoes, King Edward or Maris Piper, peeled
50 g/2 oz onions, diced
a large handful of fresh mint leaves, finely chopped
25 g/1 oz butter
½ teaspoon lemon juice
grated rind of ½ lemon
salt
chilli powder for dusting

Arguments have developed over the origins of this dish at many tables, although to my knowledge no satisfactory conclusion was ever reached. This is a wonderful way to spin out the long tropical nights, with the never-ending supply of good wine and Eastern hospitality.

1 Boil the potatoes until cooked through, then drain. Return to the pan and place on a low heat to evaporate any excess moisture and mash.
2 Add the onions, mint and butter, mixing everything together well, then blend in the lemon juice and rind. Season to taste with salt.
3 Shape the mashed potatoes into large or small patties, dust with chilli powder and serve hot or cold.
Note: This makes a wonderful accompaniment to barbecued meats and dry curries.

SPICED SAUTÉED POTATOES

For 4–6 people
Preparation time 15 minutes
Cooking time 35 minutes

450 g/1 lb small new potatoes
2 tablespoons vegetable oil
1 clove garlic, crushed
1 teaspoon turmeric
2 teaspoons ground coriander
2 teaspoons black cumin seeds
2 teaspoons caster sugar
salt and freshly ground pepper
1 tablespoon chopped parsley
1 tablespoon chopped chives

I have served this dish in my restaurant many times and the reaction from my customers has always delighted me, in that they appreciated this 'new method' of cooking new potatoes. I didn't have the heart to tell them this 'new method' was 200 years old!

1 Bring a pan of salted water to the boil, put in the potatoes and boil for 5 minutes, then drain.
2 Heat the oil in a metal roasting pan on top of the cooker over a moderate heat and fry the garlic, turmeric, ground coriander and cumin seeds for 1 minute.
3 Add the potatoes, rolling them around to coat with the oil and spices. Sprinkle with the sugar and a little salt and pepper.
4 Place in a moderate oven, 180°C/350°F/Gas Mark 4, and bake for 30 minutes, turning them from time to time.
5 Just before serving, sprinkle on the parsley and chives.

SPICED BANANAS

For 2–4 people
Preparation time 5 minutes
Cooking time 12 minutes

This is an attractive and rather unusual accompaniment to a main dish – curry or otherwise – which gives the humble banana an extraordinary flavour.

450 g/1 lb firm bananas
25 g/1 oz butter
1½ teaspoons black cumin seeds
2 tablespoons orange juice
1 tablespoon lemon juice
a pinch of chilli powder
salt

1 Peel the bananas and slice into rounds.
2 Heat the butter in a frying pan and add the cumin seeds. Sauté gently on a low heat until the seeds begin to pop, about 6–8 minutes.
3 Add the orange and lemon juice and simmer for 1 minute, stirring continuously.
4 Put in the bananas and chilli powder, stir to evenly coat the pieces and add a little salt to taste.
5 Cook for a minute or two and serve hot or cool, but not chilled.

SPICED BANANAS IN YOGHURT

For 6–8 people
Preparation time 20 minutes

4 bananas
275 ml/½ pint natural yoghurt
2 tablespoons lemon juice
2 teaspoons sugar
½ teaspoon salt
3 tablespoons desiccated coconut soaked in 3 tablespoons hot milk
1 teaspoon oil
1 teaspoon cumin seeds
1 teaspoon black mustard seeds

1 Peel and slice the bananas.
2 Pour the yoghurt into a suitable bowl and season with the lemon juice, sugar and salt.
3 Stir in the bananas and moistened coconut.
4 Heat the oil in a small saucepan and sauté the cumin and mustard seeds until the mustard seeds pop. Pour over the yoghurt mixture and blend in.
5 Serve as a side dish to any curry meal.
Note: To add a little more bite, if desired, add a pinch or two of chilli powder to the yoghurt.

FRIED VEGETABLES

For 4 people
Preparation time 10 minutes
Cooking time 7 minutes

450 g/1 lb French beans, topped and tailed
110 g/4 oz onions, diced
25 g/1 oz butter
1 tablespoon vegetable oil
1 clove garlic, crushed
a good pinch of chilli powder
1 bay leaf
¼ teaspoon turmeric
a pinch of ground nutmeg
a pinch of ground ginger
75 ml/3 fl oz chicken stock (see page 9)
salt

French beans have always been a favourite of mine and I have adapted this recipe to suite my taste for beans – that is, crisp. If, however you like your beans 'cooked through', then allow them to simmer for a few minutes longer.

1 Sauté the onions in the butter and oil on a medium heat for 1 minute.
2 Add the garlic, chilli, bay leaf, turmeric, nutmeg and ginger. Stir and cook for 1 minute longer.
3 Add the beans, stir and cook for 1 minute, then pour on the chicken stock. Bring to the boil, reduce the heat to low and simmer for 4 minutes. Season and serve immediately.
Note: You can substitute 1–2 fresh red chillies, seeds removed and diced, for the chilli powder, and if you use 1 tablespoon soy sauce and 75 ml/3 fl oz water with a pinch of sugar in place of the chicken stock this will give a totally new taste. When using soy sauce, leave out the turmeric.

STIR-FRIED CARROTS

For 4 people
Preparation time 15 minutes
Cooking time 6 minutes

Carrots are not traditionally Indonesian; they were introduced into Indonesia by the Dutch in the seventeenth century, and the Indonesians in their own inimitable style adapted the carrot to suit their particular tastes. The name associated with carrot dishes in Indonesia is wortel, *meaning carrot, and this word, although very un-Indonesian, has been borrowed from the Dutch language to describe carrot dishes.*

450 g/1 lb carrots
50 g/2 oz onions, diced
2 tablespoons vegetable oil
25 g/1 oz butter
2 cloves garlic, crushed
a good pinch of chilli powder
110 ml/4 fl oz chicken stock (see page 9)
salt

1 Peel and wash the carrots and cut them into thin 5-cm/2-inch sticks.
2 Sauté the onions in the oil and butter in a frying pan for 1 minute, add the garlic, chilli powder and carrots and cook gently for another minute.
3 Add the stock and simmer gently for 4 minutes. Season to taste with salt and serve immediately.
Note: Runner beans, cauliflower, courgettes, etc., can be cooked in a similar manner.

CABBAGE IN COCONUT MILK

For 4 people
Preparation time 15 minutes
Cooking time 10 minutes

225 g/8 oz white cabbage, shredded
110 g/4 oz onions, diced
2 tablespoons vegetable oil
¼ teaspoon chilli powder
1 teaspoon turmeric
½ teaspoon ground coriander
275 ml/½ pint coconut milk (see page 105)
225 g/8 oz waxy potatoes, peeled and cooked
salt

1 Sauté the onions in the oil for 1 minute. Add the chilli powder, turmeric and coriander and cook gently for a further minute.
2 Add the cabbage and sauté gently for 3 minutes. Pour on the coconut milk, bring to the boil and simmer for 2 minutes.
3 Cut the potatoes into cubes and add to the cabbage. Stir well and season with salt.
4 Simmer until the potatoes are warm, then serve.

SPICED BROCCOLI

For 4 people
Preparation time 15 minutes
Cooking time 10 minutes

Broccoli is known by the elaborate title of sejenis bunga kubis *in Indonesia. This recipe was given to me by an Indian lady whose family had lived for generations in Java. It has the feel and taste of India about it and goes very well with almost every plain or spiced dish.*

450 g/1 lb broccoli
75 ml/3 fl oz natural yoghurt
1 clove garlic, crushed
½ teaspoon garam masala or paprika
salt

1 Cut the stalks about 2.5 cm/1 inch down from the heads of the broccoli. Peel the stalks to expose the soft green flesh.
2 Bring a pan of salted water to the boil and cook the broccoli for 5 minutes.
3 Meanwhile, gently heat the yoghurt, garlic and garam masala or paprika in a small pan and season to taste with salt.
4 Place the broccoli in a heated bowl, spoon the sauce over and serve immediately.
Note: A good friend and a great chef served a cold version of this sauce with smoked haddock at the start of an eight-course meal in Edinburgh.

RAJAH'S CABBAGE

For 2 people
Preparation time 15 minutes
Cooking time 5 minutes

Early green cabbages are a luscious deep green and loosely packed, often with pointed heads and tender outer leaves that are ideal for this recipe. However, the later cabbages, particularly the Savoy variety, may be used, but be selective and choose only the freshest. Read this recipe through carefully before starting.

6 outer leaves of green cabbage
1 small onion, peeled and finely sliced
½ teaspoon chilli powder
25 g/1 oz desiccated coconut
a good pinch of turmeric
salt

1 Thoroughly wash the cabbage leaves and pat dry. Very carefully stack one on top of the other and gently roll into a tight tube. Cut into very fine strips with a sharp knife.
2 Heat a deep saucepan over a high heat, quickly drop in the cabbage, onion and chilli powder and give it a quick stir. Cover with a close-fitting lid and, keeping the heat high, cook for about 1 minute.
3 Mix together the desiccated coconut and turmeric and add it to the cabbage, stirring to blend the ingredients together. At this stage, judgement is more important than time. Continue stirring until the coconut releases its aroma, which it will do when it is 'cooked'.
4 Season with salt and serve immediately.
Note: If the heat is too low when the cabbage goes into the pan, then cooking will be too slow, the liquid in the cabbage will come out and the luscious green colour will be lost. A little practice may be required to achieve perfection, but the finished product is well worth a little extra effort.

FENNEL WITH PRAWNS

For 6 people
Preparation time 15 minutes
Cooking time 10 minutes

450 g/1 lb fennel, quartered and sliced
175 g/6 oz cooked prawns, shelled
3 tablespoons vegetable oil
175 g/6 oz onions, diced
½ teaspoon ground ginger
¼ teaspoon ground chilli
1-cm/½-inch slice creamed coconut (see page 105)
½ teaspoon sugar

1 Heat the oil in a large frying pan and, when hot, sauté the onions for 2 minutes.
2 Add the ginger and chilli and sauté for 1 minute longer, stirring continuously.
3 Stir in the fennel and cook for 2 minutes.
4 Add the slice of coconut and quickly blend into the fennel by stirring continuously.
5 Put in the prawns and sugar, season to taste with salt and pepper, then cook for a minute longer. Serve immediately.

VEGETABLE CURRY

For 4 people
Preparation time 15 minutes
Cooking time 25 minutes

Commonly known as Avial, *this is a lovely main dish for vegetarians. As a side dish it is usually served with dry curries and accompanying relishes.*

3 medium potatoes, peeled and cut into 4-cm/1½-inch cubes
4 carrots, peeled and diced
½ teaspoon turmeric
½ teaspoon chilli powder
175 g/6 oz French beans, topped and tailed
1 medium cauliflower
1 medium aubergine, cut into 2.5-cm/1-inch slices
3 tomatoes, quartered
50 g/2 oz desiccated coconut
275 ml/½ pint natural yoghurt
salt

1 Put the cubed potatoes and diced carrots into a deep pan and pour in enough water just to cover the vegetables, approximately 1.2 litres/2 pints. Bring to the boil and simmer for 5 minutes.
2 Add the turmeric, chilli powder, French beans and cauliflower and mix well, then add the aubergine and tomatoes and bring to the boil. Simmer until all the vegetables are cooked, about 10 minutes.
3 Add the desiccated coconut and yoghurt. Bring back to the boil, stirring well.
4 Add salt to taste and serve at once.
Note: For this fairly liquid curry you can use any vegetable, either on its own or as a combination.

Substitute 6 fresh green chillies, sliced in half, for the chilli powder (if you can get them), together with 2 or 3 slices of fresh ginger.

COURGETTE CURRY

For 2 people
Preparation time 20 minutes
Cooking time 30 minutes

225 g/8 oz courgettes, sliced
110 g/4 oz onions, diced
1 clove garlic
1 tablespoon vegetable oil
1 teaspoon cumin seeds
½ teaspoon turmeric
110 g/4 oz fresh tomatoes, chopped
1 tablespoon water
½ teaspoon cinnamon
1 small green pepper, deseeded and diced
salt to taste

1 Fry the onions and garlic in the oil for 5 minutes over a moderate heat.
2 Add the cumin seeds and fry for 5 minutes longer – be careful not to burn.
3 Add the turmeric, tomatoes and water, cover and simmer gently for 5 minutes more.
4 Add all the other ingredients, cover and continue to simmer gently for 15 minutes. Serve hot as a vegetarian dish or as a side dish.
Note: The green pepper can be replaced by 1 or 2 fresh green chillies, deseeded and diced, depending on how hot you like your food.

SPICED AUBERGINE WITH YOGHURT

For 4–6 people
Preparation time 20 minutes
Cooking time 1½ hours

1 medium aubergine
4 tablespoons olive oil
1 teaspoon black mustard seeds
110 g/4 oz onions, diced
2 fresh green chillies, deseeded and sliced
2 tomatoes, peeled, deseeded and diced
1 teaspoon mixed spices (see page 106)
1 teaspoon salt
275 ml/½ pint natural yoghurt
2 teaspoons chopped fresh parsley

1 Bake the aubergine in a moderately hot oven, 200°C/400°F/ Gas Mark 6, until soft – about 1 hour. Remove, and when cool peel and chop finely.
2 Heat the oil in a saucepan and sauté the mustard seeds until they pop. Add the onions and chillies and continue to cook for 4–5 minutes.
3 Add the tomatoes, mixed spices, salt and the aubergine and continue to cook on a low heat until all the liquid evaporates and the mixture is thick and forms a purée. Remove from the heat and set aside to cool.
4 Stir in yoghurt and parsley, chill for 2–3 hours before serving.
Note: The 2 fresh green chillies may be replaced by ¼ teaspoon chilli powder.

INDONESIAN CAVIAR

For 6 people
Preparation time 30 minutes
Cooking time 2 hours

2 large aubergines
6 tablespoons olive oil
225 g/8 oz onions, diced
1 clove garlic, crushed
1 small green pepper, deseeded and diced
4 tomatoes, peeled and chopped
1 teaspoon finely grated ginger, fresh or dried
½ teaspoon turmeric
½ teaspoon chilli powder
2 teaspoons salt
1 teaspoon mixed spices (see page 106)

A well-known cookery writer christened this dish 'Poor Man's Caviar'. Although it tastes nothing like its namesake, I have tried to recreate the aubergine purée of Indonesia.

1 Bake the aubergines in a moderately hot oven, 200°C/400°F/ Gas Mark 6, until soft – about 1 hour. Remove and, when cool, peel them.
2 Heat the oil in a saucepan and sauté the onions and garlic until golden.
3 Add the green pepper, tomatoes, ginger, turmeric, chilli, salt and mixed spices and mix thoroughly.
4 Chop the peeled aubergines finely and add to the other ingredients. Blend well.
5 Simmer the mixture gently, stirring occasionally to prevent sticking, until all the liquid evaporates and the mixture is thick.
6 Serve hot with bread as a starter or snack, or cold as a side dish.
Note: Ground ginger cannot be used in this recipe.

MUSHROOM CURRY

For 4 people
Preparation time 20 minutes
Cooking time 25 minutes

1 Wash the mushrooms thoroughly and cut into quarters.
2 Heat the oil in a deep saucepan and sauté the garlic, ginger and leeks gently for a minute or two.
3 Add the curry powder, salt and mushrooms and continue to stir over a low heat for 15 minutes.
4 Sprinkle with mixed spices, add the coconut milk and cook, uncovered, stirring continuously until the first signs of coming to the boil.
5 Remove from the heat and stir in the lemon juice. Serve immediately with plain white rice or vegetable rice.
Note: Ground ginger cannot be used in this recipe.

450 g/1 lb mushrooms
30 ml/1 fl oz vegetable oil
2 cloves garlic, crushed
½ teaspoon finely grated ginger, dried or fresh
2 leeks, washed and finely sliced
2 teaspoons curry powder
1 teaspoon salt
1 teaspoon mixed spices (see page 106)
150 ml/¼ pint thick coconut milk (see page 105)
2 teaspoons lemon juice

DRIED BEAN CURRY

For 4 people
Soaking time overnight
Preparation time 25 minutes
Cooking time 2½ hours

This dish is for vegetarians and should be served with boiled rice or bread.

1 Soak the beans in plenty of cold water overnight.
2 Drain, rinse and put the beans in a large saucepan with water to cover and 1 teaspoon of salt. Bring to the boil, cover and cook until tender. This will take approximately 1–2 hours. Drain and reserve the cooking liquid.
3 Heat the butter in a large saucepan and gently fry the onions for 5 minutes, then stir in the garlic, ginger, turmeric, mixed spices, tomatoes, chilli, mint, remaining salt and lemon juice.
4 Add the beans and stir everything together over a medium heat for 5 minutes.
5 Add 275 ml/½ pint of the reserved cooking liquid and cook over a low heat until the tomatoes and chillies are soft and the sauce starts to get thick. Serve immediately.

225 g/8 oz dried beans, any variety
2 teaspoons salt
25 g/1 oz unsalted butter
225 g/8 oz onions, finely diced
2 cloves garlic, crushed
1 tablespoon finely chopped fresh ginger
1 teaspoon turmeric
1 teaspoon mixed spices (see page 106)
175 g/6 oz ripe tomatoes, chopped
1 fresh green chilli, deseeded and finely sliced
2 tablespoons chopped fresh mint
2 tablespoons lemon juice

SPICED FRIED LEEKS

For 4 people
Preparation time 10 minutes
Cooking time 12 minutes

4–5 large leeks
50 g/2 oz unsalted butter
1 teaspoon cumin seeds
1 teaspoon turmeric
1 teaspoon finely grated fresh ginger
1 teaspoon mixed spices (see page 106)
salt

1 Top and tail the leeks, then split them from top to bottom with a sharp knife and wash thoroughly, getting rid of all soil and grit. Chop coarsely.
2 Heat the butter in a large saucepan and sauté the cumin for 1 minute, stirring.
3 Add the turmeric and ginger and continue cooking for a minute longer.
4 Put in the leeks, stir well and sauté for 5 minutes.
5 Sprinkle on the mixed spices, add a little salt to taste, cover and cook for 5 minutes longer, stirring occasionally. Serve immediately.
Note: This recipe can be made in exactly the same way, substituting onions for leeks.

INDONESIAN SPAGHETTI

For 4 people
Preparation time 20 minutes
Cooking time 10 minutes

225 g/8 oz cooked spaghetti
50 g/2 oz butter
1 large onion, diced
1 clove garlic, crushed
2 tomatoes, peeled, deseeded and diced
1 red chilli, seeds removed and finely sliced
1 good tablespoon tomato ketchup
3 eggs, well beaten
25 g/1 oz grated cheese
salt

Spaghetti does not just belong to the Italians. After all, where did they get it from? This is an interesting dish I came across on my travels; it was served with a type of beef stew. My first impression was that it looked like spaghetti carbonara, but that was where the similarity ended.

1 Melt the butter in a large frying pan and cook the onion over a gentle heat until soft, about 10 minutes, adding the garlic halfway through.
2 Add the tomatoes, chilli and spaghetti, stirring well.
3 Add the tomato ketchup, cook gently for about 5 minutes, then add the beaten egg.
4 Stir well and, when the egg starts to congeal, add the grated cheese, season with salt and mix well.
5 Serve with a main course or as a starter.

Rice Dishes

For Asians, nothing in the world can be simpler to cook than plain boiled rice. However, rice varies from batch to batch and, because of the varieties available nowadays in shops, it is difficult to know which cooking method applies to which type. Generally speaking, the rice bought in packets from shops will always carry cooking methods printed on the packets. Don't take these printed instructions as gospel as, in my experience, rice never behaves as you expect it to. In particular, I've found that rice varies in its ability to absorb water; sometimes needing more and sometimes less. Experimentation is the name of the game. I am not going to go into the merits of one rice against the other; indeed, my own preference has come about by many years in Indonesia, cooking rice as easily as one would boil potatoes. This chapter is for those who are stepping into the heart of Eastern cooking for the first time, and require a rice that will perform well and on time, without trauma. For the following recipes I have chosen converted rice. Converted rice is a long-grain rice which is more nutritious than one might think because it is steam-treated and processed before it is hulled, and so has the chance to absorb the bran's nutrients before this is discarded. It is slightly more expensive than some varieties, but it has its advantages in being quicker to cook and more nutritious (as there is also a brown long-grain rice). It has an excellent flavour and is almost foolproof.

PLAIN BOILED RICE (Nasi Liwet)

For 4 people
Preparation time 5 minutes
Cooking time 25 minutes

225 g/8 oz long-grain rice, white or brown
570 ml/1 pint water
a pinch of salt

1 Put the rice into a suitable pan, dissolve the salt in the water and pour onto the rice.
2 Bring to the boil on a high heat, turn the heat to low and simmer gently until all the liquid has evaporated, approximately 16 minutes.
3 Remove from the heat, cover with a close-fitting lid and set aside for 10 minutes.

COCONUT RICE (Nasi Gurih)

For 4 people
Preparation time 15 minutes
Cooking time 25 minutes

225 g/8 oz long-grain rice, white or brown
570 ml/1 pint coconut milk (see page 105)
1 bay leaf
5-cm/2-inch stick cinnamon
½ teaspoon grated lemon rind
a pinch of salt

1 Put all the ingredients except the rice into a suitable pan with a close-fitting lid, bring to the boil. Put in the rice and simmer gently until all the liquid evaporates. Stir gently.
2 Replace the lid and set aside for 10 minutes. Remove the bay leaf and cinnamon stick before serving.
Note: In Indonesia this basic rice dish is served on festive occasions, both family and religious, and many things will be added to it according to the area and festive occasion.

YELLOW RICE (Nasi Kuning)

For 4 people
Preparation time 15 minutes
Cooking time 25 minutes

225 g/8 oz long-grain rice, white
570 ml/1 pint coconut milk (see page 105)
½ teaspoon turmeric
1 bay leaf
2 cloves
a pinch of salt

This is another traditional festival rice dish. At Bruwah Selamatan *(breaking of fast),* Nasi Kuning *is served with an Indonesian omelette, but it is also quite acceptable for this combination to be served on any special occasion.*

1 Bring the coconut milk, turmeric, bay leaf, cloves and salt to the boil. Add the rice and simmer gently for 15 minutes or until all the liquid has evaporated.
2 Remove the bay leaf and cloves, stir gently, cover with a close-fiting lid and set aside for 10 minutes. Serve hot.

SPICED RICE (*Nasi Kebuli*)

For 4 people
Preparation time 15 minutes
Cooking time 25 minutes

225 g/8 oz long-grain rice, white
110 g/4 oz onions, diced
50 g/2 oz unsalted butter
1 clove garlic, crushed
¼ teaspoon turmeric
2 cloves, whole
2 cardamom pods, husks removed
1 bay leaf
570 ml/1 pint chicken stock *(see page 9)*

1 Sauté the onions gently in the butter in a frying pan until soft – about 5 minutes. Add the garlic and fry for a minute longer.
2 Put in the rice, turmeric, cloves, cardamom and bay leaf and fry gently for 2 minutes.
3 Add the stock, bring to the boil, turn the heat down and simmer gently for 15 minutes or until all the liquid has evaporated. Stir gently.
4 Cover the pan with a close-fitting lid, remove from the heat and set aside for 10 minutes. Remove the bay leaf before serving.
Note: This dish, by itself or with a dish of vegetables, will make an excellent ad hoc Sunday lunch or dinner party. It goes well with other dishes, for example *satay*, if you are going to entertain on a large scale. If you have any cooked pieces of chicken in the refrigerator, these can be deep-fried and served with the *Nasi Kebuli*, garnished with fried onions, parsley, chives and sliced cucumber.

SPICED RICE WITH PRAWNS

For 4–6 people
Preparation time 20 minutes
Cooking time 30 minutes

225 g/8 oz long-grain rice
450 g/1 lb prawns, cooked
50 g/2 oz unsalted butter
110 g/4 oz onions, diced
2 cloves garlic, crushed
½ teaspoon finely grated fresh ginger
4 cardamom pods, husks removed
4 cloves
5-cm/2-inch stick cinnamon
1 teaspoon ground mixed spices *(see page 106)*
½ teaspoon chilli powder
1 teaspoon salt
570 ml/1 pint fish stock *(see page 9)*
sliced cucumber and chopped parsley to garnish

1 Heat the butter in a heavy saucepan and gently fry the onions for 2 minutes.
2 Add the garlic and ginger and cook for a further minute, stirring.
3 Add the cardamom, cloves and cinnamon and cook for 2 minutes more.
4 Put in the rice and stir well. Add the ground mixed spices, chilli powder and salt and blend well.
5 Pour in the stock. Bring to a fast boil, reduce the heat and simmer gently for 15 minutes or until all the liquid has evaporated.
6 Add the prawns, fork over the rice, cover with a close-fitting lid and set aside for 10 minutes.
7 Garnish with sliced cucumber and chopped parsley before serving.
Note: Two fresh red chillies, seeds removed and finely sliced, add colour and texture and, of course, flavour to this dish. Add these at step 4.

If fish stock cubes are not available and you cannot be bothered making your own fish stock, then ordinary boiling water will do, but add the prawns at the same time as the water.

Powdered saffron may be used in place of saffon strands, but use only ⅛ teaspoon and the soaking process will not then be necessary.

SPECIAL SPICED RICE

For 4–6 people
Preparation time 30 minutes
Cooking time 2¾ hours

For the stock
1 kg/2 lb chicken
2 litres/3½ pints water
2 teaspoons salt
2 large carrots, peeled and cut into quarters
4 sticks celery, washed and cut into quarters
2 leeks, trimmed, washed and cut in half
4 cardamom pods, husks removed
10 whole black peppercorns
1 large onion, peeled
4 cloves

For the rice
450 g/1 lb long-grain rice
110 g/4 oz unsalted butter
225 g/8 oz onions, diced
½ teaspoon saffron powder
2 cloves garlic, crushed
½ teaspoon finely grated fresh ginger
½ teaspoon ground mixed spices (see page 106)
4 cardamom pods, husks removed
3 teaspoons rose water (optional)
50 g/2 oz sultanas

To garnish
50 g/2 oz toasted flaked almonds
225 g/8 oz cooked green peas
3 hard-boiled eggs, shelled and quartered

1 To make the stock, cut the chicken into six pieces, cut off and discard the 'parson's nose'.
2 Place the pieces in a large saucepan and completely cover with cold water and set aside for 2 hours. Strain off the water and discard.
3 Put the 2 litres/3½ pints of fresh water into the pan with the chicken pieces, add the salt and bring to a fast boil. Skim off any scum that forms on the surface.
4 Add all the other ingredients for the stock and simmer for 2 hours.
5 Strain the stock and measure 1 litre/1¾ pints. If there is any left over, reserve for another day. Take out the chicken pieces and remove all the flesh from the bones. Cut this into bite-sized pieces and set aside. Discard the bones.
6 For the rice, heat the butter in a large, heavy saucepan and gently fry the onions for 5 minutes.
7 Add the saffron powder, garlic and ginger and continue to cook, stirring, for 1 minute longer.
8 Add the rice, stir well, then add the ground mixed spices, cardamom, rose water, sultanas, reserved chicken pieces and stock. Stir well, bring to a fast boil, turn down the heat and simmer gently for 20 minutes, or until all the liquid has evaporated.
9 Remove from the heat, gently fork over the rice, cover with a close-fitting lid and set aside for 15 minutes.
10 Garnish with almonds, hot green peas and the quartered hard-boiled eggs before serving.
Note: Saffron strands soaked in boiling water for 10 minutes may be used in place of powdered saffron, but add them at step 8.

SAFFRON RICE

For 4 people
Preparation time 20 minutes
Cooking time 35 minutes

True saffron is fabulously expensive – each shred is a crocus stigma and each saffron crocus has three stigmas to be hand-picked and dried. It is the most delicate of condiments; unique if only for the fact that, although used in very small quantities, its power is unrivalled. It takes 75 000 crocus blooms to make 450 g/1 lb saffron, but then this delicate spice can colour several thousand times its own weight. Synthetic food colour is often used in place of saffron, or turmeric is often substituted, but unfortunately there is no substitute for the flavour of the real spice.

225 g/8 oz long-grain rice
50 g/2 oz butter
110 g/4 oz onions, diced
1 clove garlic, crushed
2 cloves, whole
2 cardamom pods, husks removed
1 teaspoon freshly ground black pepper
½ teaspoon saffron strands soaked in 1 tablespoon boiling water for 30 minutes
570 ml/1 pint hot water
½ teaspoon salt

1 Melt the butter in a saucepan and gently sauté the onions for 5 minutes. Add the garlic, cloves, cardamom and pepper and continue to cook for 1 minute longer.
2 Add the rice, mix well into the spices and fry for 3 minutes.
3 Add the saffron with its liquid and stir well, then add the water and salt and bring to the boil. Lower the heat and simmer gently for 15 minutes, or until all the liquid has evaporated.
4 Stir gently, cover with a close-fitting lid, remove from the heat and set aside for 10 minutes before serving.

SWEET LEMON AND SAFFRON RICE

For 4–6 people
Preparation time 10 minutes
Cooking time 30 minutes

225 g/8 oz long-grain rice
¼ teaspoon saffron strands
2 tablespoons boiling water
50 g/2 oz unsalted butter
6 cardamom pods, husks removed
4 cloves
5-cm/2-inch stick cinnamon
570 ml/1 pint hot water
55 ml/2 fl oz lemon juice
grated rind of 1 lemon
1 tablespoon sugar
1 teaspoon salt

1 Soak the saffron in the boiling water for 10 minutes.
2 Heat the butter in a heavy-based saucepan and gently fry the cardamom, cloves and cinnamon for 2 minutes.
3 Add the rice and continue stirring and frying for 2–3 minutes longer.
4 Pour on the hot water, lemon juice and rind, sugar, saffron and liquid and salt. Stir well and bring to a fast boil on a high heat. Reduce the heat to low and simmer gently for 15 minutes or until all the liquid has evaporated.
5 Fork over lightly, cover with a close-fitting lid and set aside for 10 minutes before serving.

Note: You may if you wish remove all the spices from the rice before serving. I personally do not, as I like the contrast and textures the spices give when being served.

SPICED SAFFRON RICE

For 4 people
Preparation time 20 minutes
Cooking time 30 minutes

1 Soak the saffron in the boiling water for 10 minutes.
2 Heat the butter in a heavy-based saucepan and gently fry the cardamom, cloves and peppercorns for 2 minutes.
3 Add the rice and continue stirring and frying for 2–3 minutes longer.
4 Pour in the hot water, add the salt, the soaked saffron strands with the liquid and the grated orange rind. Stir, bring to a fast boil, reduce the heat and simmer for 15 minutes or until all the liquid has evaporated.
5 Add the sultanas, fork over the rice, cover with a close-fitting lid and set aside for 10 minutes.
6 Serve garnished with toasted almonds and pistachios scattered over the rice.

225 g/8 oz long-grain rice
¼ teaspoon saffron strands
2 tablespoons boiling water
50 g/2 oz unsalted butter
2 cardamom pods, husks removed
2 cloves
5 black peppercorns
570 ml/1 pint hot water
1 teaspoon salt
grated rind of 1 orange
1 tablespoon sultanas

To garnish
1 tablespoon blanched sliced almonds, toasted
1 tablespoon pistachios, halved

FRAGRANT RICE

For 6–8 people
Preparation time 10 minutes
Cooking time 30 minutes

1 Bring the coconut milk with all the flavourings and spices to the boil in a large saucepan.
2 Stir in the rice, return to the boil, then turn the heat very low and cook for 15–20 minutes or until all the liquid has evaporated.
3 Gently fork over the rice, mixing in any coconut milk that has not been absorbed. Cover with a close-fitting lid and set aside to finish cooking in its own heat for 10 minutes.
4 Serve hot with any fried or spiced dish.

450 g/1 lb long grain rice, white
1 litre/1¾ pints coconut milk (see page 105)
¼ teaspoon freshly ground black pepper
1 teaspoon grated lemon rind
½ teaspoon ground nutmeg
¼ teaspoon ground cloves
2 bay leaves
2 teaspoons salt

Sweet and Sour Fish (see page 29) *with Rice with Mixed Vegetables* (see page 101) *and Fried Rice* (see page 100)

FRIED RICE (Nasi Goreng)

For 4–6 people
Preparation time 20 minutes
Cooking time 15 minutes

Nasi Goreng *is the collective description for an infinite number of differing dishes, meaning simply 'fried rice'. You can vary the ingredients to suit your taste – my favourite recipe is listed below.*

450 g/1 lb, cooked rice
2 eggs
salt
3 tablespoons vegetable oil
110 g/4 oz onions, diced
1 clove garlic, crushed
225 g/8 oz minced beef
2 rashers streaky bacon, diced
½ teaspoon chilli powder
1 teaspoon paprika
1 tablespoon soy sauce
1 teaspoon brown sugar
1 teaspoon tomato ketchup
25 g/1 oz cooked prawns

1 Beat the eggs with a pinch of salt. Heat 1 tablespoon of oil in a frying pan, pour in the eggs and cook as a thin omelette. Remove and set aside in a warm place.
2 Heat the remaining 2 tablespoons of oil in a deep pan, add the onions and garlic and fry over a gentle heat for 3 minutes or until soft.
3 Add the beef, bacon, chilli powder, paprika, soy sauce, brown sugar and tomato ketchup and sauté over a high heat for about 5 minutes until the beef is cooked.
4 Add the rice and prawns and stir well until all the rice is heated and coated with the sauce – this will take about 8 minutes.
5 Transfer to a large dish, slice the omelette into thin strips and scatter over the top. Garnish if liked with cucumber, tomatoes, fried onions and prawn crackers or crisps.

SAVOURY RICE WITH LENTILS

For 4–6 people
Preparation time 15 minutes
Cooking time 30 minutes

225 g/8 oz long grain rice
225 g/8 oz red lentils
50 g/2 oz butter
225 g/8 oz onions, finely diced
1 teaspoon ground mixed spices (see page 106)
570 ml/1 pint chicken stock (see page 9)

1 Wash the lentils thoroughly, discarding any that float to the surface.
2 Heat the butter in a suitable pan and gently sauté the onions without browning for 2 minutes.
3 Add the rice, lentils and ground mixed spices. Cook for a further 2 minutes.
4 Pour in the stock, bring to the boil, turn the heat down and simmer gently for 15 minutes or until all the liquid has evaporated. Stir carefully.
5 Cover the pan with a close-fitting lid, remove from the heat and set aside for 10 minutes, then serve.

RICE WITH MIXED VEGETABLES

For 4–6 people
Preparation time 30 minutes
Cooking time 30 minutes

225 g/8 oz long grain rice
50 g/2 oz butter
110 g/4 oz onions, diced
1 clove garlic, crushed
1 teaspoon ground mixed spices (see page 106)
570 ml/1 pint water
1 teaspoon salt
75 g/3 oz carrots, peeled and cut into 5-cm/2-inch lengths the thickness of matchsticks
50 g/2 oz green beans, thinly sliced
50 g/2 oz diced sweet peppers, red or green
50 g/2 oz potatoes, peeled and cubed
50 g/2 oz peas, fresh or frozen

1 Heat the butter in a deep pan with a close-fitting lid and sauté the onions for 3 minutes without browning. Stir in the garlic.
2 Add the rice and cook gently for 2 minutes longer, then add the ground mixed spices, water and salt. Bring to fast boil, lower the heat and simmer gently for 10 minutes.
3 Put in all the vegetables, add a little more salt if required (do not stir), put on the lid and cook gently for a further 10 minutes.
4 Remove from the heat, take off the cover and check to see if all moisture has evaporated and that the vegetables are still nice and crunchy. If there is still some liquid left, return the pan to a low heat and simmer gently until it evaporates.
5 Fork over lightly, cover and set aside for 10 minutes, then serve.

CHAPATI

Makes 16
Preparation time 30 minutes
Resting time 30 minutes
Cooking time 20 minutes

Chapatis *are an Indian unleavened bread made from fine-ground wholewheat flour. They are generally used to pick up food with and are eaten hot with all curries and savoury dishes.*

250 g/9 oz finely ground wholewheat flour (or finely sifted wheatmeal flour)
a pinch of salt
175 ml/6 fl oz water
150 g/5 oz wholewheat flour for dusting
a little melted butter

1 Sift the flour with the salt into a bowl through a fine sieve.
2 Slowly add the water, binding the flour together to form a soft dough.
3 Knead the dough for 7–9 minutes or until it is smooth. Put it into a suitable bowl, cover or wrap in plastic cling film and refrigerate for at least 30 minutes.
4 Heat a heavy cast-iron pan on a medium heat for 10 minutes, then turn the heat to low (the pan must now be very hot).
5 While the pan is heating, knead the dough again and divide into 16 balls, rolling or patting into circles. Keep your work surface well dusted

with flour, but slap off the excess flour on the *chapatis* between your hands before cooking.

6 Brush the pan with melted butter and cook the *chapati* 30 seconds on one side, then turn and cook the other side for a further 30 seconds. The bread should have light brown marks on both sides.

7 Remove the *chapati* from the pan, place it directly over the low flame and it should puff up. Turn the *chapati* over and let the other side sit on the flame for a few seconds.

8 Put onto a plate, cover with a napkin and continue.

Note: Originally, *chapatis* were placed directly on top of 'live' charcoals and it is this exposure to direct heat that makes them puff up. A low gas flame will give the same results. Making perfect *chapatis* comes with practice: if they look a little oddly shaped at the beginning, never mind, they will taste delicious.

INDONESIAN PANCAKES

For 4 people
Preparation time 5 minutes
Cooking time 20 minutes

The literal translation of Roti Jala *is 'bread casting-net'. I suppose the lacy pattern of this pancake and the way the Indonesians eat with it, wrapping morsels of food in it, together with their love of fishing, makes the name of this dish ideal.*

225 g/8 oz plain flour
a pinch of salt
2 eggs
275 ml/½ pint water
oil

1 Sift the flour and salt into a deep bowl.

2 Beat the eggs and water into the flour to make a thin batter.

3 Grease a suitable pan with oil and heat it until it starts to smoke. Dip all five fingers of one hand into the bowl of batter and let the mixture run from your fingers into the pan in a lacy pattern.

4 Turn the pancake over before it browns and cook the other side. Transfer to a wire cooling rack and let cool thoroughly before stacking.

5 Repeat the process until all the batter is used up and you will have 16–20 pancakes.

Note: At one dinner party, I served these pancakes draped over fillets of spiced fish. We spent a lot of time telling stories from our pancakes, as each one had a different picture in the pattern.

Fish Curry (see page 33) *with Chapati* (see page 101) *and Marinated Fish* (see page 29)

Relishes and Chutneys

Sambal *is the common word for any hot or spicy relish served with food in Asia. Some indeed are extremely hot and should be approached with utmost caution, as they can cause a great deal of suffering to the uninitiated. You can adjust the 'heat' of your* sambal *of course by putting in more or less chilli.* Sambals *and chutneys are usually treated a bit like our mint or apple sauces, that is they are served in a small bowl or dish and guests can help themselves with as much or as little as they like.*

Chutneys are world-renowned and there are many excellent brands on the market. As it is customary to serve chutneys with curry meals, it is a matter of personal choice as to which one to buy. However, to my surprise, chutney-making is a comparatively easy process and, therefore, the only choice now is which one to make. So for good measure I include some tried and true recipes. Serve them not only with curries but with cold and hot meats, sandwiches and salads.

COCONUT MILK

Santen *is the Javanese name for coconut milk, and this is not, as generally believed, the thin, deliciously sweet liquid found in newly opened nuts. Coconut milk is pressed from the white flesh of the nut and contains a mixture of oils and water. In Indonesia it is used to enhance and thicken sauces, adding a rich, nutty flavour which is unobtainable in any other way.*

From fresh coconut
1 coconut
425 ml/¾ pint milk or water

1 Pierce two of the 'eyes' at the top of the coconut with a strong, sharp instrument.
2 Shake out the juice. This should be drinkable in a fairly fresh coconut, but be careful as if it is too old the juice will have gone sour. If so, discard it.
3 Bake the empty nut in a hot oven for 15 minutes.
4 Lay the hot nut down, and give the centre of the nut a sharp blow with a hammer. It should break easily in two.
5 Prise the white flesh away from the hard shell and peel or scrape off the brown skin.
6 Grate the flesh finely into a deep bowl and pour in half of the milk or water and stir gently with a wooden spoon so that the gratings absorb some of the milk or water.
7 Lay a large strainer covered with muslin over a bowl and pour into it the gratings and the milk or water. Gather up the muslin and gently squeeze the gratings to extract all the milk. Place the gratings back into the original bowl, add the other half of milk or water and repeat.
Note: You should have at least 570 ml/1 pint of coconut milk. If a recipe calls for thick coconut milk, then the first squeeze is sufficient.

From desiccated coconut
350 g/12 oz desiccated coconut
570 ml/1 pint water or milk

1 Place the desiccated coconut into a liquidizer or food processor.
2 Bring the water or milk to the boil and pour half onto the desiccated coconut.
3 Run the machine for 20 or 30 seconds, then strain through a fine sieve or muslin, squeezing the coconut dry.
4 Repeat the process with the squeezed coconut and remains of the water or milk. If a recipe calls for a thick coconut milk, then the first squeeze is sufficient. If necessary, a third squeeze may be taken from the coconut to give a little extra milk.

From creamed coconut
Many shops, supermarkets and health food stores stock creamed coconut, either in compressed white slabs or jars. This can only be added at the end of recipes, after the main cooking process is completed. It then behaves like butter and can be used to thicken and flavour many dishes. On no account should the dish be reheated above boiling point.
Note: Coconut milk when stored in cold conditions will separate, with the thick cream floating to the top. This cream can be skimmed off and used as thick coconut milk when required, or you may blend it back again by standing the container in warm water and stirring.

GROUND MIXED SPICES

Spices are the essence of Eastern cooking and the ground mixed spices are sometimes added with other spices at the frying stage, but more often they are sprinkled on during the last few minutes of cooking. Once ground, they should be stored in airtight glass containers away from heat and light, and will keep all their characteristics for about two months.

If the spices are roasted lightly, you will find the flavour enhanced and the grinding easier. If an electric blender is not available, there is the traditional pestle and mortar to pound spices to a fine powder.

You may want to try as many versions of mixed spices as possible, and, if the truth be known, there is no steadfast rule about which spices to mix or how much to put in, but you may wish to begin with these examples and then gradually adapt them to suit your own individual tastes. Always store your ground spices in glass jars and an airtight lid – plastic containers tend to absorb flavour and therefore alter the strength of the spices. Don't forget to keep them away from direct heat or sunlight.

Mixed spices 1

2 tablespoons coriander seeds
1 tablespoon black cumin seeds
1 tablespoon whole black peppercorns
1 tablespoon cardamom seeds (measured without husks)
2 × 5-cm/2-inch sticks cinnamon
1 teaspoon whole cloves
½ average-sized nutmeg

1 Roast all the spices except the nutmeg separately in a small pan. As the aroma of each spice starts to fill the air, turn out on to a plate to cool.
2 After roasting, peel the cardamoms, discard the husks and measure out 1 tablespoon of the seeds.
3 Place all the roasted spices into an electric blender and blend to a fine powder. Finely grate the nutmeg and blend in. Store in airtight jars for no longer than 2 months.
Note: Ordinary cumin seeds may be used if the black ones are not available.

Mixed spices 2

4 × 7.5-cm/3-inch sticks cinnamon
1 tablespoon cardamom seeds
2 teaspoons whole cloves
2 teaspoons blades mace

1 Roast the spices separately until a strong aroma begins to permeate the air. Set aside on plates to cool.
2 Grind in a blender, or use a pestle and mortar. Store in airtight jars for no longer than 2 months.
Note: If grinding spices in a pestle and mortar, it is easier if the spices are still warm during grinding. Measure the cardamom seeds after roasting and once the husks have been removed.

Mixed spices 3

3 teaspoons cardamom seeds
2 teaspoons black cumin seeds
2 teaspoons whole black peppercorns
4 × 5-cm/2-inch sticks cinnamon
1 teaspoon whole cloves
½ nutmeg, grated

1 Roast the spices separately as in the previous recipe and grind to a fine powder. Add nutmeg.
2 Store in airtight glass jars for no longer than 2 months.

Cendul (see page 118), *Banana Pudding* (see page 117) *and Coconut Pancakes* (see page 118)

CURRY PASTE

110 g/4 oz ground coriander
50 g/2 oz ground cumin
1 tablespoon ground black pepper
1 tablespoon turmeric
1 tablespoon ground black mustard
½ tablespoon chilli powder
½ tablespoon salt
2 tablespoons crushed garlic
2 tablespoons crushed fresh ginger
wine vinegar for mixing
75 ml/3 fl oz vegetable oil

1 Combine all the spices, salt, garlic and ginger in a bowl. Add just enough wine vinegar to make a smooth, thick paste.
2 Heat the oil in a saucepan. When hot, put in the mixed spices and blend into the oil. Reduce the heat and continue to cook, stirring continuously until you see the oil separate from the spices, about 3 minutes.
3 Set aside to cool, then mix well and bottle.
Note: When a curry recipe calls for ginger, garlic and spices, this paste will be a perfect substitute. Use a tablespoon for every 450 g/1 lb of meat, fish or poultry.

HOT CHILLI PASTE (Sambal Ulek)

Preparation time 10 minutes

40 fresh red chillies, stems removed
vinegar
3 teaspoons salt

1 Put the chillies, seeds as well, into an electric blender. Add enough vinegar to keep the mass moving and blend to a paste.
2 Add salt, blend a little more and put into sterilized jars and store in the refrigerator for 3–4 weeks.
Note: In any recipe where I have used chilli powder, *Sambal Ulek* can be used instead, but use sparingly . . .

GREEN BEAN SAMBAL

For 4–6 people
Preparation time 30 minutes
Cooking time 5 minutes

225 g/8 oz fresh green beans
1 tablespoon peanut or vegetable oil
½ teaspoon garlic paste or crushed garlic
½ teaspoon sambal ulek *(see above)*
½ teaspoon salt or to taste
50 g/2 oz onions, finely sliced

1 Top, tail and string the beans if necessary. If large, cut into diagonal slices.
2 Heat the oil in a large frying pan, add the beans and toss over a high heat for about 2 minutes. Add the garlic and cook for a further minute.
3 Add the *sambal ulek* and salt and continue cooking for 1 minute. Mix well at this stage – the beans should still be crunchy.
4 Remove from heat, add the onion slices and mix thoroughly.
5 Serve immediately as a side dish to a curry and rice meal.

CAULIFLOWER SAMBAL

For 6 people
Preparation time 15 minutes
Cooking time 25 minutes

1 Cut the cauliflower into florets and blanch in salted boiling water for 10 minutes. Remove and immerse in cold water to arrest the cooking process. Drain and set aside.
2 Mash the anchovies with the salt and set aside.
3 Heat the oil in a frying pan and sauté the onions gently for 5 minutes. Add the garlic and *sambal ulek* and cook for 2 minutes longer.
4 Add the crushed anchovy and salt and stir well, then put in the blanched cauliflower and sauté quickly for 5 minutes, stirring continuously.
5 Serve with any spiced or curried dish, or salads.

1 cauliflower (approximately 450 g/1 lb)
2 anchovy fillets
1 teaspoon salt
3 tablespoons vegetable oil
225 g/8 oz onions, finely diced
2 cloves garlic, crushed
2 teaspoons sambal ulek *(see opposite)*

CUCUMBER SAMBAL

For 6–8 people
Preparation time 50 minutes

1 Peel the cucumber and slice very thinly. Put into a bowl, sprinkle with salt and let stand for 30 minutes or more.
2 Rinse with cold water and press out all the liquid.
3 Combine with all the other ingredients and toss well. Chill and serve with any curry.

1 large cucumber
150 ml/¼ pint thick coconut milk (see page 105)
1 fresh red chilli, deseeded and sliced
1 fresh green chilli, deseeded and sliced
50 g/2 oz onions, finely sliced
2 tablespoons lemon juice

COCONUT SAMBAL

For 4–6 people
Preparation time 15 minutes

Sambals *are usually served as accompaniments to the main meal or as an ingredient in the recipe. This* sambal, *with its unique flavour, complements almost any rice or salad and is a great favourite of mine.*

60 g/2½ oz desiccated coconut
1 teaspoon salt
a pinch of chilli powder
2 teaspoons paprika
2 tablespoons lemon juice
110 g/4 oz onions, diced
55 ml/2 fl oz hot milk

1 Put the coconut, salt, chilli powder and paprika into a bowl and mix well to blend all the ingredients.
2 Sprinkle this coconut mixture with the lemon juice, onions and milk, then mix well with your hands, rubbing and squeezing the ingredients together, so that the coconut is evenly moistened.
3 Transfer to a serving dish and chill before serving.
Note: One or two deseeded and finely chopped chillies, green or red, may be added just before serving.

ONION SAMBAL

For 4 people
Preparation time 10 minutes

225 g/8 oz onions, finely sliced
30 ml/1 fl oz lemon juice
chilli powder to taste
½ teaspoon salt
1 teaspoon chopped parsley

1 Sprinkle the onions with lemon juice, chilli powder, salt and parsley. Toss together lightly and chill. Serve with any type of curry.

PUMPKIN RELISH

For 4 people
Preparation time 15 minutes
Cooking time approximately 15 minutes

450 g/1 lb pumpkin, peeled and seeds removed
570 ml/1 pint chicken stock (see page 9)
1 teaspoon salt
10 g/½ oz butter
1 tablespoon desiccated coconut
2 teaspoons white wine vinegar
110 g/4 oz onions, finely diced
50 g/2 oz sweet red pepper, finely sliced

Never have I been served pumpkin at a dinner table in England. The only time I have seen other people use them is when they are carved into that familiar gap-toothed, smiling face at Halloween. Every year friends inundate me with these enormous golden orbs (having had the satisfaction of growing them as large as possible) to dispose of in some spectacular fashion. Little do they know that in Indonesia pumpkin and squash recipes are numerous.

1 Bring the chicken stock to the boil in a saucepan, put in the pumpkin and salt and boil gently until soft enough to mash. Drain. Discard the stock.
2 Mash the pumpkin while hot, stir in the butter, coconut, wine vinegar, onions and red pepper. Mix well, cool, then chill.
Note: The red pepper can be replaced by 2–3 red chillies, seeds removed and finely sliced. This dish goes well with rice and any type of curry.

Coconut Sorbet with Banana (see page 117), *Mint Granitas with Melon* (see page 122) *and Lychee Ice Cream with Grapes* (see page 123)

TOMATO AND YOGHURT RELISH

For 4–6 people
Preparation time 5 minutes

225 g/8 oz fresh tomatoes, chopped into small pieces
225 ml/8 fl oz natural yoghurt
2 teaspoons chopped fresh mint
salt and freshly ground pepper

1 Put the yoghurt and mint into a bowl, stir well, adding salt and pepper to taste.
2 Add the tomatoes, mix well and chill before serving
Note: If you can find some fresh basil, chop it and add it to this recipe before chilling overnight.

CUCUMBER AND YOGHURT RELISH

For 4–6 people
Preparation time 15 minutes

1 large cucumber
150 ml/¼ pint natural yoghurt
salt and freshly ground pepper
½ sweet red pepper, cut into fine strips
1 tablespoon chopped chives

1 Cut the cucumber into quarters lengthways, scoop out the seeds, then slice finely.
2 Put the yoghurt into a bowl, season with salt and pepper, add the other ingredients and mix well. Chill before serving.
Note: A pinch of cayenne pepper can add a little spice to this dish if desired.

APPLE RELISH

For 4–6 people
Preparation time 15 minutes
Cooking time 5 minutes

450 g/1 lb green eating apples
75 ml/3 fl oz milk
25 g/1 oz desiccated coconut
juice and grated rind of 1 lemon
110 g/4 oz onions, crushed or finely diced
½ teaspoon chilli powder
sugar to taste
salt

1 Bring the milk to the boil in a small saucepan, remove from the heat and add the desiccated coconut. Mix well and set aside to cool.
2 Peel, core and cut the apples into small cubes. Place in a bowl and add the lemon juice and rind, then mix well to coat all the cubes.
3 Add the crushed or diced onions, chilli powder and the cooled coconut and season to taste with a little sugar and salt. Mix together and chill before serving.
Note: If you have a pestle and mortar, you can crush your onions in it; otherwise chop them with a sharp knife the way you would parsley. One small, fresh red chilli, can give colour, texture and a little 'fire'.

PINEAPPLE AND APPLE CHUTNEY

For 10–12 people
Preparation time 30 minutes
Cooking time approximately 1 hour

450 g/1 lb fresh pineapple, peeled, cored and finely diced
225 g/8 oz green apples, peeled, cored and diced
150 ml/¼ pint white vinegar
350 g/12 oz caster sugar
½ teaspoon ground cinnamon
1 heaped tablespoon preserved ginger, shredded
10 g/½ oz fresh ginger, crushed
½ teaspoon chilli powder
2 cloves garlic, crushed
2 teaspoons salt
110 g/4 oz raisins

1 Put the vinegar, sugar, cinnamon, preserved and fresh ginger, chilli powder, garlic and salt into a deep enamel or stainless steel saucepan and bring to the boil.
2 Add the pineapple, apple and raisins, reduce the heat and simmer slowly for approximately 1 hour or until the chutney reaches a thick consistency, stirring occasionally to prevent burning.
3 Pour into preserving jars and cover while still warm. Store in a cool place, and serve with any curry or roast dish.
Note: This will keep for several months.

PEANUT CHUTNEY

For 2 people
Preparation time 10 minutes

175 g/6 oz salted peanuts
¼ sweet red pepper, finely diced
1 teaspoon ground ginger
1 teaspoon caster sugar
150 ml/¼ pint natural yoghurt
2 tablespoons chopped parsley
salt

This chutney must be used within hours of being made and is ideal as an accompaniment to any curry.

1 Combine all the ingredients, mix well, adding salt to taste. Chill before serving.
Note: A small piece of ginger about 2.5 cm/1 inch long, and 1 fresh chilli, seeds removed, is called for in the original recipe. If these are available, remember to crush or finely dice them before adding to the mixture.

PEAR CHUTNEY

Makes approximately 1.5 kg/3 lb
Preparation time 30 minutes
Cooking time 1½–1¾ hours

1 kg/2 lb ripe pears, peeled, cored and diced
225 g/8 oz onions, finely diced
1 large cooking apple, peeled, cored and diced
juice and grated rind of 2 oranges
juice and grated rind of 1 lemon
1 tablespoon ground ginger
1 teaspoon chilli powder
200 g/7 oz sugar
275 ml/½ pint white wine vinegar
2 sticks cinnamon, 15 cm/6 inches long, broken into halves
6 cloves
3 cardamom pods
225 g/8 oz raisins
1 teaspoon salt

It is always difficult to know what to do with the abundance of pears that appear in the garden every year. I include this recipe, not only because it goes so well with highly spiced dishes, but also because it is truly wonderful with hot or cold roasted meats served with salads – just right for those long summer days.

1 Put the onions, apple, orange and lemon juice and rind, ginger, chilli powder, sugar, vinegar, cinnamon, cloves, cardamom pods and raisins into a large saucepan. Bring to the boil, cover and simmer on a low heat for 30 minutes.
2 Add the pears and salt, then continue to cook on a low heat, uncovered, for 45–60 minutes, stirring occasionally as the chutney thickens.
3 Spoon into wide-mouthed jars, seal and store indefinitely.
Note: The ground ginger can be replaced by 25 g/1 oz fresh ginger but it must be crushed first, and 3 fresh red chillies can be substituted for the chilli powder; just remove the seeds and slice finely.

SWEET APRICOT CHUTNEY

For 20 people
Preparation time 30 minutes
Cooking time approximately 1 hour

1.5 kg/3 lb fresh apricots
720 ml/1¼ pints malt vinegar
2 teaspoons salt
2 teaspoons chilli powder
5 cloves garlic
110 g/4 oz fresh ginger, chopped
1 teaspoon mixed spices (see page 106)
450 g/1 lb sugar
110 g/4 oz sultanas or seedless raisins

1 Cut the apricots in half and discard the stones.
2 Put a little malt vinegar in an electric blender, add the salt, chilli powder, garlic and ginger and blend to a smooth paste.
3 Put the remaining vinegar into a stainless steel saucepan, add the blended mixture, mixed spices and sugar and bring to the boil. Turn the heat to low and simmer gently for 15 minutes.
4 Add the apricots and sultanas or raisins and continue to simmer until thick and syrupy – about ¾–1 hour. Stir occasionally to prevent sticking and burning.
5 Cool and put into sterilized jars. Seal airtight and store in a cool, dark place.
Note: Peaches, green apples, mangoes or other fruit may be used in place of apricots.

MINT CHUTNEY

For 4–6 people
Preparation time 30 minutes

One of the many joys of summer is the harvesting of mint and finding new and exciting uses for it. Mint has been used for many centuries as a digestive, antiseptic and appetizer – mint tea is a universal cooling drink – as well as being used in chutneys and highly spiced dishes.

2 large handfuls fresh mint leaves
6 spring onions, chopped
2 fresh green chillies, deseeded and sliced
½ clove garlic
1 teaspoon salt
3 teaspoons sugar
1 teaspoon mixed spices (see page 106)
75 ml/3 fl oz lemon juice
2 tablespoons water

1 Put everything into an electric blender and blend to a purée. Pack into a small dish, smooth over, cover and chill until required.

Note: If you do not have an electric blender, then the time-honoured custom of pounding with pestle and mortar is the only alternative. Chop everything as finely as possible and pound it a little at a time until ground to a paste.

Chilli powder can be substituted for fresh green chillies to taste. If fresh coriander leaves are available, substitute them for the mint leaves with a teaspoon of chopped fresh ginger and you have coriander chutney.

Try this chutney with any roast meat, hot or cold, or with fish or poultry.

PEANUT-COCONUT GARNISH

For 6–8 people
Preparation time 15 minutes
Cooking time 10 minutes

150 g/5 oz roasted salted peanuts
110 g/4 oz desiccated coconut
110 g/4 oz onions, finely diced
1 clove garlic, crushed
2 tablespoons oil
1 teaspoon ground cumin
1 teaspoon ground coriander
1 tablespoon brown sugar
¼ teaspoon ground ginger
1 tablespoon lemon juice

1 Sauté the onions and garlic in the hot oil for 2 minutes or until the onions are soft.

2 Add the cumin, coriander, sugar and ginger and blend the ingredients well together over a low heat.

3 Add the coconut and lemon juice and continue to cook over a low heat until the coconut turns a golden brown.

4 Stir in the salted peanuts and mix until the ingredients are thoroughly blended.

5 Remove from the heat, set aside to cool completely, then transfer the mixture to a storage jar. Store in a cool, dry place until ready to use.

Desserts

I include in this book a section based on sweets purely in deference to Western habits. Traditionally, the main meals in Southeast Asia do not include sweets or puddings. The meal would usually end with bowls of fresh fruit, which to my mind is the best possible conclusion to such high-quality food. However, superb Southeast Asian sweets and cakes do exist. They are often enjoyed as snacks and are always eaten as between-meal indulgences. These are most often made commercially and sold in shops and markets. Most of the desserts in this section I have frequently had for breakfast, as the street-vendors – each with their own characteristic cry or sound – plied their wares on our doorstep. Tantalizing aromas filled the morning air and created ravenous appetites as fried bananas, small pancakes filled with coconut, jellies and a whole range of sticky rice cakes were presented to us, all wrapped in fresh banana leaves. I have tried to reproduce as simply as possible some of the sweets and cakes from the East so they can be served according to Western fashion as the third course of a main meal. Some of these recipes will delight you and some will certainly surprise you.

COCONUT SORBET WITH BANANA

For 6–10 people
Preparation time 20 minutes
Freezing time overnight

This is an ideal way to finish an Indonesian meal.

175 ml/6 fl oz canned coconut juice
55 ml/2 fl oz pineapple juice
150 ml/¼ pint mineral water
30 ml/1 fl oz dark rum
2 egg whites
110 g/4 oz caster sugar
3 bananas

1 Mix together the coconut and pineapple juice with the mineral water and dark rum.
2 Whip the egg whites into stiff peaks, adding the sugar gradually as you go along.
3 Fold the egg whites into the juices and rum mixture and freeze overnight.
4 To serve, peel and slice the bananas, arrange them decoratively on plates, then place a ball of the coconut sorbet beside the slices.
Note: Cold chocolate sauce is delicious with the sorbet and banana.

BANANA PUDDING

For 4–6 people
Preparation time 30 minutes
Cooking time 1 hour

Kue Talam Pisang *is another Indonesian dish that requires the versatile banana leaf as a cooking vehicle. However, a soufflé or pudding basin does equally well. Actually, the cooking method is the same as for Christmas pudding.*

2 large bananas
225 g/8 oz rice flour (see note)
50 g/2 oz cornflour
a pinch of salt
425 ml/¾ pint thick coconut milk (see page 105)
50 g/2 oz sugar (white granulated or brown)
a pinch of salt

1 Thoroughly sift the rice flour, cornflour and salt into a bowl.
2 Pour the coconut milk and sugar into a heavy-based saucepan and heat gently, stirring, until the sugar dissolves. Do not boil.
3 Peel the bananas, cut in half lengthways and then in three crossways. Put these in the soufflé dish or pudding basin.
4 Mix the warm coconut milk into the flour, stirring to make a smooth batter. Pour on top of the bananas. Cover with aluminium foil and set in a large pan of hot water over a low heat for about 1 hour. When the water level drops, top up with water from a boiling kettle. Leave to cool.
5 Turn out onto a dish as you would a jelly and serve with double cream and soft fruit.
Note: If you cannot buy rice flour locally, make your own by simply grinding any rice in a coffee grinder.

CENDUL

For 4–8 people
Preparation time 30 minutes
Cooking time 20 minutes

Cendul *is by translation a thin broth with cakes or dough floating in it. In this case, the* Cendul *is used as a dessert or even as a palate-soother after any of the hot dishes.*

775 ml/28 fl oz water
50 g/2 oz arrowroot
a little green and red food colouring
175 g/6 oz brown sugar
1.6 litres/2¾ pints coconut milk (see page 105)

1 Mix 275 ml/½ pint of water into the arrowroot in a small pan. Heat gently, stirring all the time until the mixture becomes thick and clear. Divide into two bowls, colour one with a little green food colouring and the other with red.
2 Prepare a separate basin with very cold water. Hold a coarse strainer over this basin and pour into it one of the coloured arrowroot pastes. Force this mixture through the strainer with the back of a spoon into the cold water. The mixture will break up into little bean-shaped lumps. Do the same with the other coloured paste, allow to cool then drain and set aside.
3 Put the brown sugar and 75 ml/3 fl oz of water together into a small pan, heat gently until the sugar is dissolved, turn the heat up and cook until it turns a deep golden brown.
4 Remove from the heat and pour in 425 ml/¾ pint of water. Stir well, allow to cool then chill.
5 To serve, put some cubes of ice into a large clean tea towel, wrap up and crush by pounding it with a meat bat or hammer.
6 Put some of the chilled syrup into tall glasses with 2 tablespoons of arrowroot 'beans', a scoop of crushed ice and top up with coconut milk. Serve with straws or long-handled spoons.

COCONUT PANCAKES

For 4–8 people
Preparation time 1 hour
Resting time 1 hour
Cooking time 30 minutes

The Indonesian name for this dish is Kuih Dadar, *sounding a little like something from* Star Wars. *As children, sugared coconut was a great family treat and still is. For this recipe I'm afraid only fresh coconut is suitable but it is well worth the extra effort.*

1 For the pancakes, sift the flour, salt and sugar into a bowl. Add the beaten egg, then gradually beat in the milk making a smooth batter, free from lumps. Sprinkle on the orange rind, beat in and set the bowl aside for 1 hour.
2 Heat a 18-cm/7-inch frying pan over a moderate heat. Add a little oil and grease the pan well using a paper towel. Whisk the batter vigorously once again.
3 Pour in just enough batter to cover the base of the pan thinly, tilting the pan to spread the batter evenly. Cook for 1 minute, then turn the pancake over and cook the other side. Remove from the pan and lay on a wire cooling rack. Repeat the process until all the batter is used up. You should have eight pancakes.
4 For the filling, dissolve the sugar in the milk in a saucepan over a gentle heat.
5 Add the spices and salt and stir in the coconut and continue heating gently until the coconut absorbs all the milk and is lovely and moist.
6 Add the lemon juice, stir well and divide the filling equally between the eight pancakes. Roll up and lay them in a shallow ovenproof dish.
7 Brush on the melted butter, sprinkle on a little caster sugar and place these in a warm oven, 150°C/300°F/Gas Mark 2, for 10 minutes. Serve at once.

225 g/8 oz grated white coconut flesh
175 g/6 oz muscavado sugar
275 ml/½ pint milk
a pinch of ground cinnamon
a pinch of ground nutmeg
a pinch of salt
2 teaspoons lemon juice
a little melted butter and caster sugar for glazing

Pancakes
110 g/4 oz plain flour
a pinch of salt
½ teaspoon sugar
1 egg, beaten
275 ml/½ pint milk
grated rind of ½ orange
a little oil for frying

SPICED FRUIT SALAD

For 4–6 people
Preparation time 30 minutes

This fruit salad, unlike the Western version, is hot, spicy, slightly sour and has a sharp bite to it. Rujak, *as it is commonly known in Indonesia, is a great favourite as a dessert, usually made with* kendondong *– a tropical fruit with a firm, crisp flesh,* jeruk bali, *a large citrus fruit with red flesh, and mangoes, etc. This is my Western version, and friends always enjoy it – once they have recovered from the shock of finding chilli in a fruit salad!*

1 Put all the prepared fruit into a glass bowl, sprinkle with salt and pour in just enough cold water to cover the fruit. Stir well and set aside.
2 To make the dressing or *bumbu*, mix all the ingredients in a shallow bowl, using the back of a spoon to crush and dissolve the sugar. At the finish, it should resemble a thick syrup.
3 When ready to serve, drain off all the water from the fruit, pour on the *bumbu* and mix gently.

1 pink grapefruit, pomelo or ugli fruit, peeled and segmented
1 underripe mango or 2 underripe pears, peeled and diced
½ fresh pineapple, peeled, cored and diced
¼ cucumber, peeled and sliced
2 firm, crisp, green eating apples, peeled, cored and diced
a pinch of salt

Dressing
a pinch of chilli powder
110 g/4 oz soft dark brown sugar
a pinch of salt
1 tablespoon lime or lemon juice
1 teaspoon wine vinegar

INDONESIAN RICE PUDDING

For 4–6 people
Preparation time 10 minutes
Cooking time 2½ hours

110 g/4 oz short-grain rice
2 litres/3½ pints milk
225 g/8 oz sugar
4 cardamom pods
50 g/2 oz butter, cut into small squares
25 g/1 oz blanched, slivered almonds
¼ teaspoon ground cardamom
1 tablespoon rose water
¼ teaspoon nutmeg

1 Preheat the oven to 140°C/275°F/Gas Mark 1.
2 Wash the rice thoroughly, drain and put into a greased pie dish. Add the milk, sugar, cardamon pods and butter, stir well and place in the oven.
3 After 30 minutes, stir the pudding and repeat again after a further 30 minutes.
4 Add the slivered almonds and ground cardamom. Stir well and cook for a further 1½ hours or until the consistency is like porridge and the rice is well cooked.
5 Remove from the oven, half cool, then add the rose water and grated nutmeg. Stir well and serve warm or chilled in a large bowl or individual sweet dishes.

SPICED RICE BLANCMANGE

For 4 people
Preparation time 15 minutes
Cooking time 15 minutes

3 tablespoons ground rice
720 ml/1¼ pints milk
4 tablespoons sugar
½ teaspoon ground cardamom
1 tablespoon rose water
1 tablespoon blanched almonds, chopped
1 tablespoon blanched flaked almonds

1 Put the ground rice into a small bowl and add enough milk to make into a smooth cream.
2 Bring the rest of the milk and sugar to the boil, stirring with a wooden spoon. Remove from the heat and add the creamed ground rice, stirring to blend in well.
3 Return the pan to the heat and stir constantly until the mixture thickens and comes to the boil. Reduce the heat and simmer for 3 minutes.
4 Add the cardamom, rose water and the chopped blanched almonds. Stir well.
5 Pour into individual ramekins and garnish with flaked almonds. Serve warm or chilled.

SPICED COCONUT CUSTARD

For 6–8 people
Preparation time 30 minutes
Cooking time 1¾ hours

150 g/5 oz dark muscavado sugar
150 ml/¼ pint water
4 eggs
350 ml/12 fl oz thick coconut milk (see note)
175 ml/6 fl oz evaporated milk
½ teaspoon ground cardamom
¼ teaspoon ground mace
a pinch of ground cloves
1 tablespoon rose water

1 Dissolve the sugar in the water over a low heat until it forms a syrup. Set aside to cool.
2 Beat the eggs lightly, add the sugar syrup and whisk gently, pouring in the coconut milk, evaporated milk, spices and rose water. Transfer to a large jug.
3 Pour into individual ramekins. Place the ramekins in a baking dish lined with several sheets of newspaper.
4 Pour in enough boiling water to come halfway up the sides of the ramekins and place in a cool oven, 110°C/225°F/Gas Mark ¼, for 1½ hours. Remove from oven, cool and chill before serving.
Note: The coconut milk should be made by adding milk and not water to the desiccated coconut (see page 105).

MERINGUE SERRANGGA

For 4 people
Preparation time 15 minutes
Cooking time 25 minutes

The origin of this dish is a little obscure. It is believed that when my great grandfather went as a missionary to Borneo he accidentally married a Dyak chief's daughter. His Chinese cook made for the wedding feast a gigantic cake filled with fruit and custard topped with a mountain of beaten egg white. The chief was so impressed with this that, as is the custom, he went one better and gave my great grandfather a real mountain and the land around it. Hence the name Serrangga, *meaning mountain peak. It is still referred to in Dyak legend as 'the day the man brought the mountain of shimmering light'. This recipe has been slightly modified.*

2 firm, crisp, green eating apples, peeled and cored
2 large bananas, peeled
juice and grated rind of 1 lemon
40 g/1½ oz cornflour
55 ml/2 fl oz water
2 large eggs, separated
110 g/4 oz sugar
55 ml/2 fl oz milk
a little icing sugar for dusting

1 Slice the apples and bananas thinly and arrange in alternate layers in an ovenproof dish, sprinkling each layer with a little lemon juice.
2 Put the cornflour into a bowl, add the water and mix until dissolved.
3 Whisk in the egg yolks, sugar, milk and lemon rind. Transfer to a saucepan and heat gently, stirring continuously until the custard becomes thick and smooth. Pour over the fruit.
4 Beat the egg whites until stiff and spoon over the top of the custard. Sprinkle with icing sugar and bake in a preheated 220°C/425°F/Gas Mark 7 oven for approximately 5 minutes or until the top is crisp and golden. Serve hot or cold.

COCONUT CAKE

For a 25-cm/10-inch square cake
Preparation time 30 minutes
Cooking time 1½ hours

At home, we took the grated, rich flesh of coconuts picked straight from the tree, then ground it finely on a stone slab to get a mixture much like finely ground almonds, but because of the rich coconut liquid it was much wetter. I have adapted this recipe for desiccated coconut but if fresh coconuts are available, then you will need two of medium size.

225 g/8 oz desiccated coconut
225 g/8 oz rice flour
110 g/4 oz self-raising flour
2 teaspoons baking powder
¼ teaspoon ground cardamom
¼ teaspoon ground cloves
¼ teaspoon ground cinnamon
720 ml/1¼ pints water
4 eggs, separated
450 g/1 lb caster sugar
1 tablespoon rose water
110 g/4 oz blanched almonds, finely chopped

1 Preheat the oven to 160°C/325°F/Gas Mark 3.
2 Line a deep 25-cm/10-inch square cake tin, or two loaf tins, with buttered greaseproof paper.
3 Sift both flours, the baking powder and ground spices three or four times through a fine sieve. Set aside.
4 Put half the desiccated coconut and half the water into an electric blender and blend on high for 1 minute. Empty the blender and repeat the process with the other half of coconut and water.
5 Using a large bowl, beat the egg yolks, 400 g/14 oz of the sugar and 2 tablespoons of the coconut mixture until light and creamy. Add the remaining coconut and beat well.
6 Stir the sifted flour and spices into the coconut mixture, add the rose water and nuts and blend in.
7 Beat the egg whites to a soft snow and, while beating, sprinkle in the remaining sugar and continue beating until thick and glossy.
8 Fold into the coconut mixture, pour into the prepared tin and bake for 1¼–1½ hours. When well risen and golden, insert a skewer into the centre – if it comes out clean, it is cooked.
9 Remove from the oven, allow to half cool in the tin, then lift out and cool completely on a wire cooling rack.

MINT GRANITAS WITH MELON

For 4 people
Preparation time 30 minutes
Freezing time overnight
Cooking time 10 minutes

I can remember baking hot days, sitting on sandy shores in the shade of giant palm trees, sucking giant shaved ice balls flavoured with fruit syrups.

1 Bring the water and caster sugar to the boil, add the lemon rind and simmer gently for 10 minutes.
2 Remove from the heat and add the mint. Cover and infuse for 10 minutes. Strain and set aside to cool.
3 Add the bottle of white wine, orange and lemon juice and mix well with a few drops of green food colouring.
4 Pour into a suitable container and freeze overnight.
5 Remove, break up and mix the mint *granitas* with a fork and then replace in the freezer.
6 Slice each melon in half and remove the seeds.
7 Pile spoonfuls of the mint *granitas* into the centre of each half of melon and decorate with crystallized mint leaves. Serve at once.

Note: To crystallize mint leaves, pick the small tips of the mint only. Brush with egg white and dip in caster sugar until completely coated. Place on a metal baking sheet and freeze.

Mint Granitas is delicious served on its own, or with any other fruit as a starter, palate cleanser or sweet.

2 small ogen melons
75 ml/3 fl oz water
110 g/4 oz caster sugar
pared rind of 1 lemon
a large handful of fresh mint
1 bottle dry white wine
juice of 1 orange
juice of ½ lemon
a few drops of green food colouring
crystallized mint leaves to garnish

LYCHEE ICE CREAM WITH GRAPES

For 6–8 people
Preparation time 30 minutes

1 Purée the flesh from the lychees, adding the lemon juice.
2 Bring the milk to the boil.
3 Cream the egg yolks with the sugar, then add the boiling milk, stirring well.
4 Return the mixture to the pan and heat gently, stirring continuously, until the custard coats the back of the spoon.
5 Add the vanilla essence and the lychee purée and set aside to cool.
6 Whip the double cream until stiff and fold into the lychee and custard mixture.
7 Pour into a suitable container and freeze. Serve with black or green grapes that have been left in the freezer ovenight.

Note: A terrine is a good freezing mould for this ice cream. Once frozen, simply immerse the sides of the terrine in warm water for a few seconds, then remove, wipe dry and tip out onto a flat surface. Cut into slices and serve.

Toasted almonds and orange segments are an interesting addition to this dish as a garnish.

1 kg/2 lb fresh lychees, peeled and stoned
juice of ½ lemon
275 ml/½ pint milk
4 egg yolks
150 g/5 oz caster sugar
1 teaspoon vanilla essence
300 ml/11 fl oz double cream
450 g/1 lb black or green grapes

Glossary

Anise *(Junten Manis)* This is also known as sweet cumin. In the East, anise flavours green figs, jam, vegetables and fish curries. Buy anise in small quantities as it quickly loses its strength.

Cardamom *(Kapulaga)* Genuine cardamom is costly and has many inferior relatives. It is a strongly scented, slightly bitter Indian spice, best bought whole in green or pale brown pods the size of a little fingernail. Roughly break these open before adding to a dish.

Cayenne Pepper *(Cabé)* This is made from ground, dried chillies, and is originally from Cayenne in French Guiana. It is very hot and rather delicious.

Chillies *(Lombok)* There are many varieties of chilli, ranging from the fiery 'birdseye' to the insipid sweet capsicum. Fresh chillies, whether red or green, are savage. Don't take a large bite to try it out, for even a little nibble could have you dousing your head in buckets of cold water. After cutting them, wash your hands, as the juice should not come into contact with the eyes. Chilli powders are dried, ground chilli – sometimes red, sometimes black – and they do vary enormously. They can be pungent, mild, tasty or absolutely vicious, and only by experience can you know what you are getting.

Chillies are not so much a taste as a chemical reaction. It is said that they stimulate appetities, lower the body temperature and bring about a peace of mind.

Cinnamon Sticks *(Kaju Manis)* These are curled, paper-thin pieces of the bark of the cinnamon tree, packed one inside the other.

Cloves *(Tjengken)* Sweet and warm, this is *the* scent of the Spice Islands. Cloves have been used in all manner of ways since their discovery, particularly for toothache because of their numbing quality.

Coriander *(Ketumbar)* This is a basic ingredient of all Indonesian curries. It has a warm, faintly orangey fragrance and is best bought as seeds, which are ground and then roasted lightly before use. The leaves are often used as a flavouring in soups or as a garnish. They look like a flat-leaved parsley, but the flavour is strong and an acquired taste. Coriander is easy to grow if planted in spring or summer, but protect it well as snails adore it.

Cumin *(Djinten)* This is essential in curries. Its scent is powerful, sweet, a little oily and unmistakable, which is just as well as it is often confused with caraway.

Fennel Seeds *(Jiji Adas)* These have a sweet aniseed flavour. A few seeds chewed after dinner aid digestion and sweeten the breath.

Fenugreek This Indian seed is sometimes used in small quantities in curry powders. European commercial curry powders carry an over-emphasized bland smell of this spice, which is rather unpleasant.

Garlic *(Bawang Puteh)* The Indonesian variety of garlic is similar to the European, although smaller and having no more than four or five cloves to the bulb.

Ginger *(Djahe)* Wherever possible, the root of the ginger plant, which is Indian or Chinese in origin, must be used for cooking. Often called green ginger, it should be young and juicy, although the ones for sale in this country tend to be old and fibrous. When a 'slice' of green ginger is called for, it means an average cross section. Prepare it the same way as you would garlic.

Noodles *(Mie)* When not called vermicelli, this usually refers to Chinese dried wheatflour noodles.

Nutmeg *(Pala)* This is so well known, it needs no explanation. The grated whole nutmeg will always give a better flavour than the ready-ground.

Onions *(Bawang Merah)* Small Bombay onions are generally used in Asian cooking and not the large Spanish variety. They are sometimes available to us as shallots and if possible should be substituted in any recipe that calls for onions. One Spanish onion equals four shallots.

Peanuts *(Katjang Tanah)* Many Indonesian recipes call for peanuts in their sauces. These should always be bought raw and gently dry-fried before being crushed for use in the sauce. Crunchy peanut butter is a good substitute but does not have the same flavour.

Peppercorns *(Lada)* For the recipes in this book, they can be either black or white, but they must always be freshly ground.

Sesame Oil *(Minyak Bijan)* Bottles of this oil can be bought in most supermarkets nowadays. It is expensive and concentrated: the thicker and browner the oil, the more aromatic it is. The oil is made from toasted sesame seeds and is often used for flavouring rather than frying, as it tends to burn very easily. The pale yellowish oil that appears in many recipes from the East is quite different from the brown: it is odourless and light in texture.

Soy Sauce *(Ketjap)* Nearly every shop carries a commercial brand of soy sauce. There are basically three types: light, dark and sweet. The labels will indicate which variety they are.

Spring Onions *(Daun Bawang)* These are small and slim, like miniature leeks. They have a mild taste and are quite delicate. All of the onion can be used.

Turmeric *(Kunjit)* This is not as pretty and as golden as saffron, but is a deep yellow ochre that turns curries with dark spices to a warm mahogany colour. The flavour is pungent and sometimes bitter. Use sparingly.

Index